THE GREAT ASCENT

THE

The struggle for economic

GREAT

development in our time

ASCENT

ROBERT L. HEILBRONER

HARPER TORCHBOOKS
The University Library

HARPER & ROW, PUBLISHERS
NEW YORK, EVANSTON, AND LONDON

For Amy and Louise

ACKNOWLEDGMENTS

A number of people have been kind enough to read this book and to give me the benefit of their criticisms, favorable and otherwise. In particular I am happy to thank Albert O. Hirschman, Theodore Geiger, Harry Braverman, John Fischer, Eli Ginsberg, and Peter L. Bernstein for comments on the manuscript, while absolving them of any responsibility for the arguments of the text. As so often before, I am deeply indebted to my wife's careful editorial scrutiny, and as always I find my greatest obligation to my most scrupulous critic, Adolph Lowe.

CONTENTS

MAP   6

I THE MEASURE OF THE CHALLENGE   7
The Impact on America. The terms of the challenge.

II THE TABLEAU OF UNDERDEVELOPMENT   23
The map of underdevelopment. The 100 nations. Geography and climate. Resources. The faces of underdevelopment.

III THE SHACKLES OF BACKWARDNESS   38
The problem of productivity. The problem of social attitudes. Workers, entrepreneurs, and bureaucrats. The great transformation. The quicksand of population growth. Vicious circles.

IV THE GREAT RESOLVE   61
The initial impetus. Lopsided development. Political and economic resentments. The focus of aspiration.

V THE ENGINEERING OF DEVELOPMENT   73
The hidden potential. The peasant problem. Industrialization. An over-all view: the take-off.

VI THE SPEED OF DEVELOPMENT   88
Population control. Capital productivity. Raising the flow of savings. Channels of trade. The flow of private capital. Foreign aid. The total impact.

VII THE SOCIAL COST   122
The developers. Social tensions. The political possibilities. The logic of collectivism. The possibilities for communism.

VIII THE CHALLENGE TO THE WEST   142
The threat of isolationism. Selective support. The premises of political policy. The internationalization of foreign aid. Reform at home. The choice before America.

INDEX   159

5

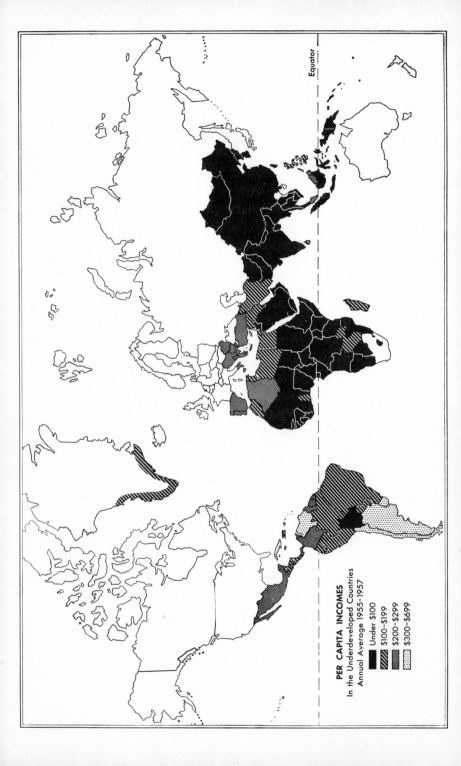

PER CAPITA INCOMES
In the Underdeveloped Countries
Annual Average 1955-1957

Under $100
$100-$199
$200-$299
$300-$699

Equator

THE
MEASURE
OF THE
CHALLENGE

I

Nothing is more remarkable, when we compare the happenings of our time with those of only a generation ago, than the extraordinary change in the scale of world events. It is as if the familiar newsreel of history had given way to a gigantic Cinerama, as if the once dark wings of the theater were now illumined by an immense extension of the screen on which history is projected to us. And this sense of change in scale is not merely an illusion based on our receding distance from the past. During the middle years of the twentieth century we have actually been spectators at an unprecedented enlargement of human affairs, an enlargement which may well appear in the future as one of the great watersheds in human history.

Thus it is instructive to compare the scope of events twenty-five years ago with that of today. To the West, the chain of happenings leading up to World War II seemed to reach around the entire world. Yet what strikes us now is not how large, but how circumscribed and restricted was the theater of history of those days. While Europe and America hovered at the brink of a supreme historic involvement, at least to Western eyes, the far larger and more populous areas of the East and South mainly slumbered. India, plucking feebly at its British bonds, resembled a drugged Gulliver. China, in itself comprising a quarter of the world's population, suffered military rape in a surrender of total exhaustion. Latin America, aside from its dreary chronicle of coup and exploitation, was to all intents and purposes an historic zero. Africa languished in oblivion. The Near East rotted amid general indifference.

It was not merely by virtue of their passive relationship to the approaching war that these areas were largely excluded from the screen of history. Of far more significance was their passive existence in times of peace. It was not for nothing that the newsreel of events was almost exclusively concerned with Russia and Europe and America, for in the rest of the world a profound torpor reigned. If the populations of the great continents of the East and South suffered, their sufferings effected little or no noticeable change in the character of twentieth-century civilization. If the peoples of Asia and Africa and Latin America entertained individual aspirations, these were without impact on their collective condition of life. Insofar as "history" consists of a shared political and social and economic self-consciousness which becomes part of the biographies of millions of human beings, helping to shape those biographies and to give them a common purpose, it can fairly be said that most of the underdeveloped world had no history.*

It is the filling-in of this vacuum which accounts for the near-explosion of history in our times. And it is not merely the increased activity, much less the violence and disorder which are now so prominent in the East and South, that signals this new era. Violence and disorder are not new to these lands. What is new, what propels these areas into history of a kind which cannot any longer be described by the traditional chronology of a personal struggle for rule, is a central process visible throughout the newly awakened areas. This is the process of economic development—of a world-wide struggle to escape from the poverty and misery, and not less from the neglect and anonymity, which have heretofore constituted "life" to the vast majority of human beings.

It is not mere rhetoric to speak of this attempted Great Ascent as the first real act of world history. Certainly in size and scope it towers over any previous enterprise of man. For over one hundred nations, economic development means the chance to become a national entity, to live in the chronicle of recorded events. For over two billion human beings, it means something at once humbler and infinitely more important: the chance to become a personal entity, simply to live. And over and beyond this immense impact of development on the lives which are being led

---

* As E. H. Carr has written: "It is only today that it has become possible for the first time even to imagine a whole world consisting of peoples who have in the fullest sense entered history and become the concern, no longer of the colonial administrator or the anthropologist, but of the historian." *What Is History?* (New York, Alfred A. Knopf, 1962), p. 199.

9

today looms its incalculably larger impact on the lives to be led tomorrow.

For the Great Ascent is not merely a struggle against poverty. The process which we call economic development is also, and in the long run primarily, a process through which the social, political, and economic institutions of the future are being shaped for the great majority of mankind. On the outcome of this enormous act will depend the character of the civilization of the world for many generations to come, not only in the poor and struggling nations, but in the rich and privileged ones as well. Whatever the outcome of the Cold War—indeed, whatever the outcome of a Hot War—more and more will civilization, or what is left of it, reflect the emergent societies of the newly incorporated parts of the world.

The impact on America

Hence the advent of economic development has galvanized the Old World of the West and North no less than the New World of the East and South. For the rush of the history-making process into a vastly larger area has placed these Northern and Western regions in a radically altered setting. To Russia, as well as to the United States and Europe, the immense historic potential of the developing New World has added a new dimension to geographic existence, opened a new horizon of popular consciousness, and, above all, posed a new spectrum of problems for political decision.

Nowhere has this secondary impact of development exerted a more profound influence than in the United States.

In part this has reflected a spontaneous reaction to the human spectacle of the Great Ascent itself. The upsurge of aspirations from the hitherto voiceless and hopeless has come to us as a cry from the depths; the panorama of misery and desperation visible on the faces of the Arabs, Indians, Africans, and Bolivians, who stare at us from the pages of magazines and television screens, has shocked us like a glimpse into the inferno.

Equally important have been the more considered reactions of our national leaders. Human sympathies aside, it has been clear that the United States could hardly ignore the challenge of those areas which were not only "developing" their economies but forming the institutions of their future societies. As the stalemate with Russia has grown more durable, it has become increasingly evident that the global contest of ideologies and power systems was likely to be decided, not by the default of either side, but by the drift of events among the still fluid societies of the developing world. Thus both moral concern and national self-interest have plunged us, at first hesitantly, then with mounting commitment, into support for economic development.

To be sure, the response has not been unmixed. There have been accusations of "squandering" American wealth for "wasteful purposes" and squabbles over the operation of foreign aid programs. No administration, Republican or Democratic, has yet succeeded in obtaining from Congress the full measure of foreign aid which it has sought. And yet what is remarkable in retrospect is not how little has has been accomplished but how much. It is difficult to believe today, when the promotion of economic development

11

has become a major concern of American foreign economic policy, that not less than twenty years ago it was possible to laugh away the very idea of international economic assistance as "giving milk to the Hottentots." A comparable enlargement and redirection of public interest in so short a period of time would be hard to find. Whatever else may be charged against the American reaction to the problems of this century, neither niggardliness nor lack of human concern can be rightfully attributed to our response to the challenge of economic development.

And yet the American response to the challenge of development has been seriously—even dangerously—inadequate. This is not because our personal sympathies or our national generosity could have been still greater. The shortcoming is much more important than that. What has been missing from the American response is the indispensable ingredient of understanding. It is a failure to see the Great Ascent as it is, and not as we imagine it to be.

To put it differently, the inadequacy of our response derives from our tendency to see the Great Ascent in American terms, to interpret its propensities, its capabilities, its characteristics within the framework of American economic and social and political experience. At its most naïve, this tendency reveals itself in a picture of the Ascent as a kind of global process of Americanization, a slow but steady evolutionary climb in which the people of Egypt and India and Bolivia become, little by little, more "like ourselves." Reading about development in the popular magazines and newspapers, we learn of the warm response of simple villagers to the unassuming friendliness of our Peace Corps representatives and of their admiration for the self-evident superiority of American techniques and equipment, and we are led to believe that, were it not for the machinations of the communists and the mistakes of our diplomats, there would be a natural gravitation toward American ways, a spontaneous embrace of American ideas.

This is not, to be sure, the view held by those who actively deal with the problem of development. Our government officials, university scholars, and foundation experts do not see development in the easy setting of a picture story in a magazine. They are deeply aware of the "differentness" of other cultures and of the often limited relevance of American mores or institutions for those cultures. They do not expect, or even wish for, development in terms of an export of American life.

Yet even among these sophisticated groups, a specifically American point of view colors the prospect of the Great Ascent. In part it is visible as a tendency to stress the socially constructive and annealing aspects of development. In part it is apparent in the tacit assumption that the political processes of development are discussable in an American political vocabulary. In part, again, it shows itself in the unthinking premise that rapid economic growth in an underdeveloped area will generate the same social and political contentment as it does in America. In short, despite its greater degree of "realism" and its far wider command of facts, the sophisticated American view shares with the popular view a disregard of the possibility that the propensities, capabilities, and characteristics of the

13

Great Ascent may be far removed from our own experience —may be, in fact, highly un-American.

Curiously, this American approach to the problem of development has a good deal to recommend it on the surface. It encourages our goodwill, our enthusiasm, our willingness to tackle a formidable challenge. It establishes a natural congruence between our support for development and our position in the Cold War, thus enabling us to come to uncomplicated moral judgments in our support of development for humanitarian purposes.

Hence one hesitates to cast doubts on attitudes which serve to rally us to the cause of a great and immensely important struggle. The trouble is, however, that the American view of development, for all its serviceability at the moment, ill prepares us for what lies ahead. It enables us to be "for" development today because much of what development portends for tomorrow is invisible from the American vantage point. It promotes a frame of mind and a set of policies which may do well enough for the next few years, but which will not do for the next fifty years, when the Great Ascent truly begins to dominate the tenor of world history. In a word, our present conception of development gives rise to actions and attitudes which have every virtue but that of being proved right in the long run.

The terms of the challenge

The purpose of this small book is to help us form another attitude to the Great Ascent—an attitude which, hopefully, will stand the test of the future with more resilience than our present one. Because such an attitude is much more ambiguous, demanding, and problematical than our prevailing one, an ardent enthusiast for economic development might find the tenor of these pages negative, discouraged, and discouraging. Nothing could be further from their purpose. The basic theme of this book lies in the belief that the Great Ascent is a supremely important enterprise which must command the hopes and efforts of every advanced nation. But little is gained—indeed, much can be lost—by centering those hopes on and directing those efforts to an illusion. If the Great Ascent is to succeed, and if America and the West are to succeed in adjusting themselves to its volcanic disturbances, it is imperative that we see the process as clearly and objectively as possible.

This means that we must look at development, not from the American standpoint, from without, but from the standpoint of the developing countries themselves, from within. And the difference is not merely a matter of geography. The boundaries that must be crossed are those of accustomed habits of thought, of unexamined assumptions, of comfortable social and political and economic limitations, all of which may be valid enough for the consideration of American problems but which fail to illumine the vaster problems of the emerging currents of world history.

The chapters that follow seek to describe some of the intellectual and ideological boundaries that must be crossed before we can truly penetrate the continents in which the Great Ascent is being staged. But it may help us if we commence, however abruptly, with a few warnings concerning the problems to be encountered.

1. *Economic development is not primarily an economic but a political and social process.*

Looking at development from our American viewpoint, we can scarcely help but see it as a process similar to that by which a depressed area, such as Wilkes-Barre or West Virginia, climbs out of temporary difficulties. That is, we naturally picture the sequence of economic development as a steady accumulation of wealth and a slow but growing expansion of incomes and employment. In so doing, however, we tend to overlook the fact that this kind of strictly *economic* development requires as a precondition the existence of a society in which wealth *can* be accumulated and in which incomes and employment are *capable* of being progressively enlarged.

But it is precisely this kind of society which is lacking in the underdeveloped areas. The critical fact about the underdeveloped countries is that they are not "economies" in the American sense of the word—which is to say that they do not yet have the institutions, the habits, the foundation of skills and wealth which are preconditions for a long, sustained economic climb.

Economic development, in its initial stages, is the process by which such societies are created. Much of early development is, accordingly, pre-economic. It is concerned with the shaping of attitudes and the creation, forcibly or otherwise, of workable institutional structures. All of this requires far-reaching social change, and this social change, in turn, requires for its inception the mobilization of powerful political energies. Thus we deceive ourselves when we think of economic development in the pallid terms of

16

economics alone. It is only by a profound social and political / transformation that the Great Ascent will get into motion, | and the momentum of the Ascent will itself inaugurate still further social and political change.

2. The political and social changes required for economic development are apt to be revolutionary in nature.

A second American misconception about development is that it is an evolutionary process. That is, the Great Ascent is regarded as a process in the course of which an established social order is propelled toward greater well-being, rich and poor benefiting alike, although perhaps not in equal degree.

Unfortunately, this is not an accurate description of the political dynamics of development. Inherent in the necessary reorganization of the social and economic structure of a backward nation is a reorganization of its *class structure*. Power and wealth, privilege and disprivilege are apt to undergo radical shifts, endangering, even threatening to eliminate, previously dominant interests at the expense of new and ambitious claimants.

Thus at the heart of the development process lurks a revolutionary potential—revolutionary not in the sense of a gradual redistribution of power and wealth such as accompanied the Industrial Revolution, but in the sense of a drastic, rapid, and painful redistribution such as accompanied the French or Russian revolutions.

We are not used to thinking in such violent political terms. When it is called to our attention that the Great Ascent is not apt to move rapidly unless there is a mobilization of political power in fresh hands, we imagine—and, indeed, publicly espouse—such changes under the name of government "reform." But the strains of the development process do not facilitate reform—i.e., the peaceful transfer of power from one point on the political spectrum to a neighboring point. On the contrary, the widening rifts and inescapable class frictions of the development process favor the discontinuous transfer of power from one position along the spectrum to another distant and often hostile position.

Thus the process of development displays revolutionary overtones with which an essentially conservative nation grapples with difficulty. America may favor certain kinds of "revolutionary" changes in the world, but these are not likely to be the kinds associated with the Great Ascent.

3. *Economic development is not a process which breeds social contentment.*

Yet another underlying American assumption about development is that once it is set in motion it will bring about a gradual decline in social tensions and an increase in the morale and contentment of the population. This too is an expectation in which we are apt to be sorely disappointed. For the mechanics of economic development are not such as to make possible an appreciable rise in basic living standards for most backward areas for a very long period of time. Instead, development is apt to be characterized by a growing gap between expectations and achievements—that is, by an increased awareness of insufficiency and a decreased tolerance of both poverty and privilege. For the underlying masses, development is apt to be a time of awakening hostilities, of newly felt frustrations, of growing impatience and dissatisfaction.

Then, too, among the more literate and educated portions of the nation development also exacts its price. The inevitable social rearrangements, the dissolution of old standards of value, the resentments aroused by a class of political, economic, and social *arrivistes,* the wild enthusiasm and black despair of the growing corps of semieducated intellectuals—all these disruptive factors also add their influence to the typical environment of the development process. It is a mistake to picture the Great Ascent as a time of growing social harmony. It is more likely to be a time of increased disharmony and discontent.

4. *The Great Ascent is not assured of success.*

Of all our assumptions concerning economic development, the most characteristically American is that economic development cannot fail. We cannot readily imagine the possibility that the upshot of a generation of effort on the part of the underdeveloped nations may terminate, not in the exhilaration of victory, but in the exhaustion of defeat.

Yet, taking into account the obstacles in their way, the likelihood is very great that for the majority of nations now attempting the long climb the outcome in our time will be defeat. In much of tropical Africa, most of the Near East and northern Africa, in many parts of Central and even South America, very possibly in the crucial regions of India and Indonesia, the next ten to twenty years of arduous effort are not apt to produce anything like a "self-sustaining climb." While a few nations may register substantial gains, in a far greater number the mass of the population will conclude their initial stage of the march very little, if any, higher than their starting elevation.

This does not mean that these nations are permanently consigned to poverty and backwardness. The very effort toward development will change the fabric of life in these areas irrevocably and irreversibly. The sacrifices and achievements, even if they will not immediately alter the level of average existence, will advance the day when that level will perceptibly begin to mount. But the timetable of development is apt to be much longer and to proceed much slower than our hopes for it. To be realistic, our outlook must take into account the likely inability of development in our generation to produce anything that will resemble our expectations of success.

5. *The price of development is apt to be political and economic authoritarianism.*

The immense institutional transformations, the necessary stimulus of powerful political wills, the revolutionary potential, the social friction, the arduousness of the prospect, all point to a single conclusion. It is that the price of development is apt to be the exercise of authoritarian power, both political and economic. While the form of the power may vary from nation to nation, here having a left-wing, there a military-nationalist complexion, here displaying totalitarian excesses, there some degree of tolerance, in most developing nations sooner or later the inherent stresses of the climb are likely to result in a centralized directorship of effort if the Ascent is to be made at all. Strong-man governments and collectivist economic techniques are apt to be the accompaniments of development in many backward areas—not as mere excrescences of, but as necessary conditions for, an effort great enough to sustain the enormous process.

Unfortunately, however, even the most thoroughgoing control over the social and economic energies of a backward nation may yet not bring about development at a sufficiently rapid pace to close the gap between expectations and accomplishments. Hence it would be wise to anticipate as well a rise of diversionary activities of a supernationalistic or military nature as a safety valve for frustration. It is a bitter prospect, but local war or dictatorship or both may be the only tools of social discipline capable of keeping the columns of the Ascent from falling into total disorganization.

These aspects of the development process place the Great Ascent in a very different light from that in which we are accustomed to viewing it. They imply that the realities of development are utterly unlike the average American conception of them. More sobering yet, these prospects imply that American national policy toward development is still far from realistic and that, however commendable our sympathies and generosity, even they have been marshaled for an ideal which does not exist.

This does not mean that our sympathies and support are therefore misplaced or that we should turn our backs on development. The point, rather, is that development, as an enormous extension of world history, places us in a situation the full meaning of which we have yet squarely to confront. In a sense we can no more turn our backs on the Great Ascent, even if we wanted to, than we could ignore a new Ice Age, were the polar caps again to begin their descent. Development is here, as a fundamental reality of our times, and the true challenge facing America is to adjust to it *as* a reality and not as a sentimentalized or wishful process.

What alternatives may be open to us, how we may adapt our policy and our outlook to this new and painful comprehension of the situation, is a matter we must defer for the moment. For we have yet to understand the manner in which these unexpected aspects of development are rooted in the development process itself. And for this we must understand the actual mechanism of the Great Ascent. We cannot begin to formulate an adequate response to the challenge of economic development until we have gained a close acquaintance with it—not as we imagine it to be, but as it is. Hence let us turn now to a view of the underdeveloped world, seeking to acquaint ourselves first with underdevelopment as a human reality.

THE
TABLEAU OF
UNDER-
DEVELOPMENT

II

To begin to understand economic development we must have a picture of the problem with which it contends. We must conjure up in our mind's eye what underdevelopment means for the two billion human beings for whom it is not a statistic but a living experience of daily life. Unless we can see the Great Ascent from the vantage point of those who must make the climb, we cannot hope to understand the difficulties of the march.

It is not easy to make this mental jump. But let us attempt it by imagining how a typical American family, living in a small suburban house on an income of six or seven thousand dollars, could be transformed into an equally typical family of the underdeveloped world.

We begin by invading the house of our imaginary American family to strip it of its furniture. Everything goes:

beds, chairs, tables, television set, lamps. We will leave the family with a few old blankets, a kitchen table, a wooden chair. Along with the bureaus go the clothes. Each member of the family may keep in his "wardrobe" his oldest suit or dress, a shirt or blouse. We will permit a pair of shoes to the head of the family, but none for the wife or children.

We move into the kitchen. The appliances have already been taken out, so we turn to the cupboards and larder. The box of matches may stay, a small bag of flour, some sugar and salt. A few moldy potatoes, already in the garbage can, must be hastily rescued, for they will provide much of tonight's meal. We will leave a handful of onions, and a dish of dried beans. All the rest we take away: the meat, the fresh vegetables, the canned goods, the crackers, the candy.

Now we have stripped the house: the bathroom has been dismantled, the running water shut off, the electric wires taken out. Next we take away the house. The family can move to the toolshed. It is crowded, but much better than the situation in Hong Kong, where (a United Nations report tells us) "it is not uncommon for a family of four or more to live in a bedspace, that is, on a bunk bed and the space it occupies—sometimes in two or three tiers—their only privacy provided by curtains." [1]

But we have only begun. All the other houses in the neighborhood have also been removed; our suburb has become a shantytown. Still, our family is fortunate to have a shelter; 250,000 people in Calcutta have none at all and simply live in the streets. Our family is now about on a

[1] *Social Aspects of Urban Development,* Committee on Information from Non-Self-Governing Territories, March 10, 1961, p. 129.

par with the city of Cali in Colombia, where, an official of the World Bank writes, "on one hillside alone, the slum population is estimated at 40,000—without water, sanitation, or electric light. And not all the poor of Cali are as fortunate as that. Others have built their shacks near the city on land which lies beneath the flood mark. To these people the immediate environment is the open sewer of the city, a sewer which flows through their huts when the river rises."[2]

And still we have not reduced our American family to the level at which life is lived in the greatest part of the globe. Communication must go next. No more newspapers, magazines, books—not that they are missed, since we must take away our family's literacy as well. Instead, in our shantytown we will allow one radio. In India the national average of radio ownership is one per 250 people, but since the majority of radios is owned by city dwellers, our allowance is fairly generous.

Now government services must go. No more postman, no more fireman. There is a school, but it is three miles away and consists of two classrooms. They are not too overcrowded since only half the children in the neighborhood go to school. There are, of course, no hospitals or doctors nearby. The nearest clinic is ten miles away and is tended by a midwife. It can be reached by bicycle, provided that the family has a bicycle, which is unlikely. Or one can go by bus—not always inside, but there is usually room on top.

Finally, money. We will allow our family a cash hoard of five dollars. This will prevent our breadwinner from

---

[2] "The Cauca Valley," unpublished World Bank memo by George Young. (With the kind permission of the author.)

experiencing the tragedy of an Iranian peasant who went blind because he could not raise the $3.94 which he mistakenly thought he needed to secure admission to a hospital where he could have been cured.[3]

Meanwhile the head of our family must earn his keep. As a peasant cultivator with three acres to tend, he may raise the equivalent of $100 to $300 worth of crops a year. If he is a tenant farmer, which is more than likely, a third or so of his crop will go to his landlord, and probably another 10 percent to the local moneylender. But there will be enough to eat. Or almost enough. The human body requires an input of at least 2,000 calories to replenish the energy consumed by its living cells. If our displaced American fares no better than an Indian peasant, he will average a replenishment of no more than 1,700-1,900 calories. His body, like any insufficiently fueled machine, will run down. That is one reason why life expectancy at birth in India today averages less than forty years.

But the children may help. If they are fortunate, they may find work and thus earn some cash to supplement the family's income. For example, they may be employed as are children in Hyderabad, Pakistan, sealing the ends of bangles over a small kerosene flame, a simple task which can be done at home. To be sure, the pay is small: eight annas—about ten cents—for sealing bangles. That is, eight annas per *gross* of bangles. And if they cannot find work? Well, they can scavenge, as do the children in Iran who in times of hunger search for the undigested oats in the droppings of horses.

[3] *New York Times Magazine*, April 30, 1961.

And so we have brought our typical American family down to the very bottom of the human scale. It is, however, a bottom in which we can find, give or take a hundred million souls, at least a billion people.* Of the remaining billion in the backward areas, most are slightly better off, but not much so; a few are comfortable; a handful rich.

Of course, this is only an impression of life in the underdeveloped lands. It is not life itself. There is still lacking the things that underdevelopment gives as well as those it takes away: the urinous smell of poverty, the display of disease, the flies, the open sewers. And there is lacking, too, a softening sense of familiarity. Even in a charnel house life has its passions and pleasures. A tableau, shocking to American eyes, is less shocking to eyes that have never known any other. But it gives one a general idea. It begins to add pictures of reality to the statistics by which underdevelopment is ordinarily measured. When we are told that half the world's population enjoys a standard of living "less than $100 a year," this is what the figures mean.

The map of underdevelopment

What we have gained thus far is largely a tourist's view of underdevelopment, indeed perhaps a tourist's stereo-

---

* Such an estimate is, of necessity, highly conjectural. It takes in only 300 million of India's population and 50 million of Pakistan's, a charitable figure. It includes 50 million Arabs and 100 million Africans, a large underestimate. From South and Central America's poverty it adds in but another 50 millions. The remainder of the billion can be made up from mainland China alone. And we have kept as a statistical reserve the Afghans, Burmese, Indonesians, Koreans, Vietnamese—nearly 200 million in all, among whom is to be found some of the worst poverty on the face of the globe.

type. The very sharpness with which the grinding poverty strikes us is itself testimony that we are still looking at the scene with American eyes—that we are seeing it from a vantage point different from that of the underdeveloped lands themselves. Hence if we are to shake off the sense of an alien scrutiny, we must begin to enter within the framework of underdevelopment itself. Obviously, we cannot acquire the feeling of life in these areas as if it were our life. But we can begin to pierce the surface of things by looking for the causes of this ubiquitous poverty. What lies behind the squalor and want which, with only local variations, provide the great central theme of the underdeveloped lands?

The 100 nations

It will help us to acquire an understanding of their common plight if we now spread out a map of underdevelopment and examine it. Such a map, to be completely accurate, would have to be considerably larger than can be shown on the facing page, for there are over one hundred nations and perhaps fifty territories that must be marked on it. The list runs the alphabetical gamut from Afghanistan to Zanzibar.* Nonetheless even a general overview reveals a number of significant facts.

Perhaps what strikes us first, when we look at the map,

* The classification of underdeveloped countries is at best somewhat arbitrary and the income divisions uncertain. We do not, for instance, count Russia as a backward nation, even though its per capita income might classify it as such. Were we to include its more backward regions, many of which lie to the east and south, the beltlike impression of the map would be further intensified.

is the diversity which characterizes the underdeveloped nations. In size and shape, in terrain and ecology, in political development and history there seems to be no common denominator to their condition. At least two underdeveloped nations—Brazil and China—are bigger than the United States; while three others—El Salvador, Lebanon, and Albania—would not together fill up West Virginia. Some are almost empty: Libya, with an area half the size of India, has a population smaller than the Bronx; others are fantastically crowded: Java, roughly the size of Alabama, has a population equal to one-third of the United States. Some, like China, are communist; some, like India, are "socialist"; some are capitalist; and some, like Saudi Arabia, have been described as "rushing madly from the eleventh century into the twelfth."

But if the first impression is one of diversity, when we look again at the map, an obvious but important common characteristic strikes us. It is that underdevelopment is largely concentrated in the Eastern and Southern continents: Africa (including the Near East), the land mass and archipelagoes of Asia, and the great pear-shaped expanse of South America with its Central American stem. This does not mean there is no underdevelopment elsewhere. Europe has severely underdeveloped areas in Spain and Portugal, in Yugoslavia, southern Italy, Greece, and the Black Sea countries. Oceania has its primitive islands. Greenland has a per-capita income of $100. Parts of Canada, even a few pockets of the United States, can be called underdeveloped.

There is no doubt, however, that the great core of the problem lies in the land areas of the East and South. For

Latin America as a whole the per-capita income is between $300 and $400; for Asia entire it is between $50 and $100; for Africa and the Middle East perhaps less.

Geography and climate

Is there a reason for this geographic massing of underdevelopment? One possible explanation occurs to us immediately. It springs from the fact that most of the poorer nations are wholly or partly in the tropics. Can their poverty be traced to this simple cause?

It is curious that this question, which seems so open to empirical investigation, is in fact far from simple to analyze. Not many years ago the prima-facie "evidence" made the climatic theory of underdevelopment virtually the prevalent explanation of economic backwardness. To some, the lush vegetation suggested that agriculture was virtually effortless and that the stimulus of a more grudging nature was therefore lacking. By others the heat was blamed for the chronic "laziness" of the natives. Or, again, the moist, disease-bearing terrain was thought to be inimical to sustained effort.*

Today we are somewhat more chary of ascribing underdevelopment to the influence of climate alone. To be sure, there are parts of the world where the heat is simply debilitating: not many years ago in Azizia in Tripolitania a

* A less widely advertised theory (although still held in certain quarters) has attributed underdevelopment to the "childlike" mentality of the nonwhite races. The extraordinary strides made by Japan and the enormous (if tragic) effort mounted by China should effectively controvert the view that mass poverty has an anthropological rather than a social base.

temperature of 132° was recorded in the shade. But such locales are the exception rather than the rule. Most of the tropics are not *that* hot, and even when the heat is fierce, it is frequently concentrated during certain hours of the day or months of the year. In addition, some tropical locales have shown vigorous economic growth, such as the Queensland region of Australia, or for that matter Washington, D.C., where summer service has traditionally been classified by the British Foreign Office as a "tropical" assignment.

This is not to brush aside the serious adverse effects of tropical heat (and of the disease-bearing attributes of humid and warm terrain). What is difficult is to separate out the sheerly climatic from the cultural factors, or to demonstrate with certainty the degree to which climate has produced nondevelopmental cultures.

As Dr. Benjamin Higgins, an authority on economic development, has written:

The attitude toward work, leisure, and income in Australia seems much the same from subtropical Darwin, where summer heat is more intense than in most equatorial countries, to chilly Hobart, with its ten-month-long winter and cool summers. Nor is there any significant difference in attitudes or productivity between Indonesians living at sea level and those living in the invigorating climate 4,000 feet up in the mountains.[4]

And to reinforce the difficulty of ascribing backwardness to climate alone, let us remember that not all underdeveloped countries are tropical. Korea has all the rigors of a

[4] *Economic Development* (New York, W. W. Norton, 1959), pp. 266-67.

temperate climate, as do much of Peru, Bolivia, highlands Africa, or northern China.

A more sophisticated investigation into the relationship between climate and economic backwardness might concern itself with rainfall. Much of the problem of the African Continent revolves around its inability to secure for itself an adequate share of the precipitation which annually falls on the earth's surface. Along the great northern strip of African coast, the Arab peoples have for centuries contended with a rainfall that is sporadic and insufficient, while large areas of tropical Africa alternately wash away under torrential downpours or parch under none. Asia too has had to adjust to an unfavorable distribution of annual rainfall: the great monsoons provide the critical source of water for all of South Asian agriculture and when the monsoons are late, the crops die in the fields.

Yet South America as a whole has no such problem. Nor did northern Africa always present a desert appearance. Better tilled, irrigated, and tended, it was the granary of the ancient Roman Empire. Hence, as with climate, the pattern of rainfall provides at best only a partial explanation for underdevelopment. In a few areas of the world, these two factors can be charged with presenting an environment too arduous to permit the accumulation of a surplus on which a more materially advanced civilization might be built. (The same is true, of course, of the extreme frigid zones.) Yet a global view of underdevelopment— a view which embraces the great plains of Mongolia as well as the jungles of Malaya—would be hard-pressed to attribute economic backwardness to these factors alone.

What is certain, of course, is that adverse climate and

insufficient rainfall pose obstacles for which unusually large economic efforts will be needed. But given this effort—given air-conditioning, water storage, irrigation on a large enough scale—the deficiencies of nature can be repaired, as witness the economic progress of both Australia and Israel. The tropics and the deserts will always have to reckon with and adapt to their geographic liabilities, but there is no reason why many of these regions cannot, on that account alone, eventually join the ranks of the more prosperous nations of the world.

Resources

If climate and rainfall give us only a partial insight into the causes for underdevelopment, the geographic approach to the problem at least suggests a second important factor to which we must pay heed: the availability of resources. Surely the presence of good soil or healthy forests or useful mineral deposits must be propitious for economic progress, and conversely we would expect that the poorer countries of the world were those which, by an accident of geography, were deprived of these benefits.

Unquestionably the availability of resources plays a role in the general map of underdevelopment. The author of a recent survey of Africa writes: "If there is one physical generalization for which a strong case can be made in tropical Africa, it is that good soils are the exception. Most of the soils are no better than the poorest mid-latitude soils; some are poorer, and all are more easily impoverished than enriched." [5]

[5] George Kimble, *Tropical Africa* (New York, The Twentieth Century Fund, 1960), I, p. 73.

Much of Africa is held back by its poor soil. The North, of course, suffers from totally infertile sand, and the tropical regions from earths that compact to the hardness of concrete or that tear away in the violent rainstorms: in Agulu, Nigeria, there is a gully one mile square and five hundred feet deep which has expanded its area fourfold in only six years.

It is not only Africa which suffers from this basic handicap. A great deal of the rain-forest soil of the South American Continent is also much less suitable for raising crops than its luxuriant forest cover would suggest. Across large areas of Asia, as well, the soil is also wanting: vast tracts of India are arid, while in China the land has long since been deforested and much of it overworked.

Not only an absence of good soil, but an absence of resources of other kinds can be found to hamper most areas of the underdeveloped world. Navigable rivers, promising hydroelectric sites, accessible deposits of coal and iron, of manganese, tin, bauxite, and the thousand and one raw materials of modern industry are more often than not lacking from the balance sheets of many, perhaps most, of the nations at the lower end of the world's income scale.

And yet, just as climatic conditions proved at best only a partial explanation of backwardness, so we can attribute to a lack of physical resources only a subsidiary role in causing underdevelopment. For one thing, some of the poorer countries are actually rich in resources. Indonesia, for example, is blessed with a fertile volcanic soil and has much underground wealth. South America has vast arable lands and great mineral potentials; Africa boasts huge reserves of subsoil treasure. And in many other nations what best describes the situation is not so much that resources are lacking, as that their presence is simply unknown. Typical is the case of Libya, which, until a few years ago, could have been written off as a nation almost bereft of any of the gifts of nature. Today Libya is known to be the site of tremendous oil deposits. In nearly every underdeveloped nation, a scientific inventory of available wealth has never been undertaken for lack of both skills and money: they are "poor" in resources because no one has yet systematically looked for them.

Equally important is that known *potential* resources exist in many areas, provided that economic development will bring them into being. A dam across the Niger River can create thousands of new acres of arable land for Nigeria. A dam across the Awash River in Ethiopia can make that valley one of the richest in all Africa. The irrigation of desert land around the Mediterranean can restore the ancient granary of Rome. The scientific treatment of soils in India or Pakistan has already begun to bring back to life land which was dead.

Without doubt the uneven allocation of the gifts of nature will make development much more onerous and expensive in some areas than in others. It will certainly influence the direction which development will take: encouraging animal husbandry here and rice culture there, making coal the most economic source of power in one area, oil in another, atomic power in a third. The pace and pattern of change must inevitably reflect the variety of natural habitats in which it must take place. But viewing the problem as a whole, there is no reason to consign the great bulk of the underdeveloped world to permanent poverty because of a tragic and uncorrectable decree of nature.

The faces of underdevelopment

A brief glance at resources and climate has not unlocked the riddle of underdevelopment. If it offers cogent reasons why some areas have remained backward, it cannot answer the question for others. China, for example, is not a victim of geographic discrimination. Neither is much of South America. Neither are at least large areas of Africa. Rather, a review of the anomalous and not clearly understood relationship between nature and underdevelopment calls our attention to the *historic*—that is, the social and cultural—reasons for economic backwardness. Speaking in the large, economic underdevelopment is not so much a reflection of nature as of human attitudes and institutions.

The point is important, for it calls our attention to the fact that development is not in any sense a "natural" process. It is, on the contrary, a process which has been realized only in a small portion of the world where cultural and political history have combined to bring about an extraordinary and atypical encouragement to certain types of economic behavior. The roots of economic growth in the West reach very deep into the origins of the Western outlook and the permutations of Western social and political history.[6] Economic development in the West was the final

[6] For a suggestive discussion of some of the behavioral "causes" of development, see David McClelland, *The Achieving Society*, Van Nostrand, Princeton, N.J., 1961.

link in a long chain, many links of which are missing in the Eastern and Southern background.

We shall dwell at some length on these missing preconditions for "natural" development in the backward areas. But our preliminary survey of the physical map of underdevelopment, although it does not lead us to the ultimate reason for stagnation, does at least serve to point up an important aspect of the problem. This is the wide diversity of conditions with which economic development must contend. Variations in climate and resources—compounded by variations in local customs and institutions—make of the actual work of development a many-faceted rather than a universally similar task. Bolivia, for example, must cope with the problems of high-altitude plateaus, Brazil with those of sea-level jungles. In Hong Kong the basic aspect of underdevelopment is urban; in Afghanistan it is rural. In India a major problem is the cow, for here lives a third of the world's cattle population eating up man's subsistence and immune from effective economic utilization because of religious custom; in Ghana it is swollen shoot disease, which threatens the cocoa plant on which Ghana must depend for its major export earnings.

Thus from country to country the face of underdevelopment changes. Starting from a common poverty, sharing —as we shall see—common bonds of backwardness, each must nonetheless find its unique avenue of development and cope with its unique disadvantages. As Paul Hoffman, Director of the United Nations Special Fund, has summarized it succinctly: "A hundred nations, a hundred problems."

THE
SHACKLES OF
BACKWARDNESS

III

It is well that we begin our examination of economic development with a recognition of this diversity of problems, for it inculcates a healthy skepticism against panaceas. More than that, it begins to indicate, from country to country, what is feasible and what is not: in this diversity of underdevelopment are the hard facts of life for a development economist, a UN committee weighing the merits of a request for technical assistance, or the governments of the one hundred nations themselves.

Yet it would be as misleading to stop our analysis of underdevelopment here as to have concluded it with our first composite picture of its poverty. For despite their critical differences, all of the one hundred countries also display important resemblances. If they face physical and natural obstacles of the greatest variety, they are nonetheless hobbled in the first instance by common shackles of a social and economic kind. Heretofore we have paid attention to the characteristics which differentiate one under-developed country from another. Now we must study even more closely the problems which are common and central to all of them.

The problem of productivity

Once we start to look for resemblances in the various areas of the underdeveloped world, one common handicap springs to sight immediately. It is the fact that human labor in all of these nations is so pitifully unproductive—that a day's toil, often far more back-breaking than the equivalent day's work in the West, produces so heartbreakingly little.

We see this particularly in the sector which is the very foundation of all the underdeveloped economies: agriculture. In the United States one farmer typically supports about twenty-four non-food-producing citizens. Compare this with the situation in Africa: "The productivity of African agriculture is still so low," writes Dr. Kimble, "that it takes anywhere from two to ten people—men, women and children—to raise enough food to supply their own needs and those of *one* additional—non-food-growing—adult."[1]

Or take the situation in that life-and-death crop of the East: rice. The table below shows the difference between the productivity of rice fields in the main Asiatic countries and those of the United States and Australia:

[1] Kimble, *op. cit.*, I, p. 572 (italics added).

Rice Yield per Hectare[2]
(100 kilograms)

	1955
United States	34.3
Australia	45.9
Burma	14.8
China (1954)	24.7
India	12.6
Indonesia	16.5
Thailand	14.3
Philippines	11.9
Vietnam	12.3

What is true of rice can be found true of nearly every crop. In soybeans, for instance, the United States is roughly twice as productive per acre as China or Indonesia; in tobacco it is nearly three times as productive as the Philippines. "One of the most distressing shocks to the foreign economic advisor when he first goes on mission to an underdeveloped country," writes Professor Higgins, "is the discovery that the most important local agricultural product . . . cannot compete in the free market with imports from advanced countries. Thus one finds Louisiana rice competing with native rice in the Philippines, imported dates underselling the inferior homegrown dates in Libya, California oranges competing with the small, bitter native citrus fruits in the Riau Archipelago of Indonesia."[3]

And if we compare the relative productivities, not of hectares of land, but of human labor, the contrast is even more striking. An American farmer spreads his labor over

[2] From Higgins, *op. cit.*, p. 16.
[3] *Ibid.*, p. 17.

50 to 200 acres of land; an Asian or South American farmer pours all his energies into two or three. Thus human productivity may be as little as one two-hundredth of that in an economically advanced country.

Why is agricultural labor in the underdeveloped world so unproductive? The very discrepancies in the scale of agriculture in the advanced and backward nations provide an answer.

What has been called "postage stamp cultivation" marks the pattern of farming throughout Asia and the Near East, and in much of South America and Africa. Not the farm, but the plot, is the standard unit of cultivation. Even when large landlord estates exist, they are typically subdivided into a crossword puzzle of miniscule holdings cropped by tenants. John Gunther, writing of India twenty years ago, describes the situation vividly:

There is no primogeniture in India as a rule, and when the peasant dies his land is subdivided among all his sons, with the result that most holdings are infinitesimally small. In one district in the Punjab, following fragmentation through generations, 584 owners cultivate no less than 16,000 fields; in another 12,800 acres are split into actually 63,000 holdings. Three-quarters of the holdings in India as a whole are under ten acres. In many parts of India the average holding is less than an acre.[4]

That was twenty years ago, but the situation is not significantly remedied today, and it is mirrored in many other underdeveloped lands.

Many causes contribute to this terrible division and subdivision of land. In some countries it is the custom of inheritance which Gunther mentions. In others it is attrib-

[4] *Inside Asia* (New York, Harper & Brothers, 1939), p. 385.

utable to feudal landlord systems in which peasants cannot legally own or accumulate their own land. In still larger part it is due to the pressure of too many people on too little arable soil, aggravated by enormous concentrations of landholdings in the hands of the upper classes. To many of these causal factors we shall have reason to turn again. But at this stage what we must notice is that, whatever the causes, the result is the same: agriculture suffers from a devastating lack of productivity brought about by grotesque man-land ratios.

Thus the overcrowding of the land gives rise to a *technical* condition which tragically curtails the output of crops from a given area of soil. For peasants working their tiny strips cannot efficiently utilize—nor could they possibly afford—the physical, mechanical, and chemical means by which agriculture in the West attains its rich returns. On the miniscule farms of the backward lands reapers and binders and sowers are totally uneconomic. Worse yet, because the peasant earns no investable surplus he cannot even exchange his wooden plow for a steel one, or substitute chemical fertilizer for animal or human dung. Indeed, even animal fertilizer is seldom applied; it is used instead as the slow-burning fuel over which the peasant cooks his bowl of rice. Nor is assistance available in the form of draft animals; a grim joke used to be that the Indian villager hitched his plow to the village bull, the Chinese hitched his to his wife. We can summarize all these paralyzing and debilitating lacks in a single concept: the low level of agricultural productivity is largely due to an inability to apply capital to the productive process.

This impoverishing absence of capital is by no means confined to agriculture. On the contrary, the problem pervades every underdeveloped economy from top to bottom. It is for lack of capital of every sort, not just for lack of capital on the land, that the underdeveloped nations are unable to produce adequate incomes. What these nations lack is not a supply of human labor or, in most cases, at least some resources which could be turned to account. Rather, what lacks are the machines, the power lines, the engines, the cranes, warehouses, factories, generators by which men and resources can be given the capacity to produce more than the tiny flow of output which nature yields to bare hands and primitive equipment. This is one principal reason why in 1959, for instance, when an average American worker produced $3.90 worth of goods in an hour, his Japanese counterpart produced only 40 cents' worth. And Japan is, by the standards of the underdeveloped countries, a capital-rich, highly productive economy.

This deep and ubiquitous problem of the insufficiency of capital is a matter on which we shall later dwell at some length, for clearly here lies a vital element in the prescription for economic development. But at this juncture, while we are seeking only to identify the common defects of the underdeveloped continents, it is enough that we identify the problem. If a low level of productivity is the universal economic attribute of underdevelopment, a fearful shortage of capital is its well-nigh invariable cause.

The problem of social attitudes

And yet this economic handicap is not the ultimate cause of underdevelopment. For the shortage of capital itself

43

testifies to a still deeper problem. This is the absence of those social attitudes and institutions which create capital. That is, the lack of capital directs our attention to the all-important fact that the economies of the underdeveloped world are not capital-generating. In some important structural way these economies must be different from the economies of the West, capitalist and communist alike.

What is that difference? We begin to find it when we now examine not the physical but the social attributes of the underdeveloped lands. Let us commence by considering the predominant social type of these lands—the peasant cultivator who comprises 70 to 80 percent of the populations of all the backward areas.

What do we mean by a "peasant cultivator"? Emphatically we do not mean a farmer. A farmer, particularly as we meet him in the United States, is essentially a businessman of the land. He is price and cost conscious, quick to adjust his output to the signals of the marketplace. He is technically minded and ready to alter his practices if something demonstrably better comes along. He is, for all his traditional ties to the land, very much an economic man.

The peasant presents a sharp contrast to the farmer. He does not normally reckon in terms of the plus and minus of balance sheets. He does not readily shift from this crop to that as prices change. He is not technically trained or innovation-minded. To him, the world of nature is fixed and immutable; it is to be propitiated rather than vanquished.

Thus Dr. Alvin Hansen writes of such peasant attitudes in India:

Often village opinion is hostile to ... new developments, and unless there is continual prodding, a relapse back to traditional practices is likely. This is certainly not surprising. An illiterate community with traditional cultural and religious convictions, firmly implanted from generation to generation, cannot easily be shunted over to a modern view of social values. Innovations that run counter to established dogmas and beliefs are feared lest they might anger various deities.... Innovations might bring upon the helpless villagers scourges, pestilence, floods and droughts. ...

Agricultural practices are controlled by custom and tradition. A villager is fearful of science. For many villagers insecticide is taboo because all life is sacred. A new and improved seed is suspect. To try it is a gamble. Fertilizers, for example, are indeed a risk unless scientifically applied and with just the right amount of moisture. To adopt these untried methods might be to risk failure. And failure could mean starvation.[5]

This does not mean that the peasant is forever tied to the past. When he is convinced of success, he will change his ways. As Dr. Arthur Lewis has pointed out, Gold Coast farmers, reputed to have been the laziest in the world, switched over en masse from subsistence agriculture to cocoa production when it was profitable to do so, and other economists have emphasized the response of Malayan and Ceylonese cultivators to changes in the relative prices of crops available to them. Thus it would be wrong to picture the peasant as devoid of business incentives or locked in an unshakable embrace with tradition.

But the testimony of endless teams of technical assistance workers, of agricultural experts and anthropologists

[5] *Economic Issues of the 1960s* (New York, McGraw-Hill Book Co., 1960), pp. 157-58.

warns us that the pace of peasant change in the ordinary instance is painfully slow.[6] And here Dr. Hansen's observations provide an insight into the peasant's motivations. The cultivator of the soil is not just mulish or stupid. He is operating in a world in which there is no margin for error, no room for maneuver. Against the logic of a science he does not understand, he opposes the logic of the past which has permitted him to stay alive. And sometimes he is right. In a study of the impact of innovations prepared by UNESCO we read of the unexpected vindication of old ways in the face of efforts to bring change and growth:

In Burma, deep ploughing introduced by European agricultural experts broke up the hardpan that held the water in the rice fields. The weeding of rubber plantations reduced the sap. The new tomato, which the Burmese were persuaded to grow because it was more productive, had a flavor they did not like. In Turkey experts trained abroad persuaded some of the younger peasants to remove the stones from their tilled land; when the grain sprouted, the fields of the old men had a better crop, since in that dry climate, the stones served the function of retaining moisture.[7]

Such wry miscarriages of advice should not be magnified out of proportion. In the vast majority of cases, when the peasant refuses to change his ways, he is tragically mistaken. Yet it makes more understandable the fact that change comes slowly in the peasant world, much more slowly than is needed if the Great Ascent is to move at more than a snail's pace.

[6] Cf. *Cultural Patterns and Technical Change*, ed. Margaret Mead (New York, New American Library, 1955), pp. 177-94.
[7] *Ibid.*, p. 186.

Workers, entrepreneurs, and bureaucrats

It is not only in a reluctance to change agricultural ways that we find social attitudes constituting an impediment to economic change. In the industrial sector—among those who work in and direct the enterprise of the underdeveloped nations—we find similar obstacles.

Take, for instance, the raw working force with which the new factories must be run. Eugene Black, President of the World Bank, has described their situation graphically:

The migrant to the city is perhaps the most cruelly treated by the historic transformation going on in the underdeveloped world. Away from the familiar ways of his native village, he is plunged into a bewildering, formless, insecure life, requiring a whole new set of attitudes towards life and work. If he is lucky enough to get a factory job, he is likely to find factory discipline irksome and pointless. If it is no great problem to teach him to operate a machine, often there is no common language with which to introduce him to such sophisticated ideas as quality control or the terms of a labor contract. Away from work he is more often than not herded into a wretched slum and exploited by the large, permanent world of beggars, vagrants, refugees, petty criminals, and the like who manage somehow to survive on the fringe economies of the cities of the underdeveloped world.[8]

Hence the worker, like the peasant, is not easily transformed into a member of a modern economic system. Unused to thinking of factory work as a permanent way of

[8] *The Diplomacy of Economic Development* (Cambridge, Harvard University Press, 1960), pp. 10-11.

47

life, certainly unused to the idea that it might offer the prospect of a slowly rising standard of living, he accepts the often noisome conditions of factory labor as one might accept a temporary prison sentence. "In the least developed areas," reads a recent economic report, "the worker's attitude toward labour may entirely lack time perspective, let alone the concept of productive investment. For example, the day labourer in a rural area on his way to work, who finds a fish in the net he placed in the river the night before, is observed to return home, his needs being met. The worker in an urban area who receives an increase in pay works less and goes back to his native village so much the sooner." [9]

These attitudes of inertia and resistance before the demands of an industrial society are by no means confined to the humbler classes of society. "A common psychological obstacle to economic achievement," continues the economic report, "is the fact that much higher status tends to be associated with landownership or government position or professional or intellectual activity than is enjoyed by the business-man, engineer, mechanic, agronomist or some other type of person concerned directly with material production." [10] Thus in the least developed lands the more privileged classes frequently display as much obduracy before economic development as do the peasant and simple laborer. The rich have always counted their assets in terms of gold, jewels, houses, land, and do not easily learn to count as "wealth" an ugly factory or printed stock certificates. The able have always gravitated to the

[9] *Report on World Social Situation,* Department of Economic and Social Affairs, March 9, 1961, p. 79.
[10] *Ibid.,* p. 80.

48

law, to letters, to the ministries of government, and do not take quickly to the idea of making their careers in "vulgar" undertakings. Significantly, of the many students from underdeveloped lands studying in the United States, only 4 percent are interested in that fundamental problem of their homelands—agriculture.[11] More than that, in societies in which power and status are based on land, the rise of a mercantile or industrial class is viewed with suspicion. Let us recall the bitter fight between the old aristocracy and the new manufacturers in France in the eighteenth century and in England in the early nineteenth century when we blandly assume that "wealth is wealth" and that landowners can easily metamorphize into or identify their interests with industrial capitalists.

And then, too, even among the small industrial class, the prevalent orientation toward money-making itself is different in a typical Asian or African or Latin-American nation from our own. The psychology of most businessmen is not that of the Western entrepreneur. It is more that of the bazaar merchant. Not large-scale production and long-term return, but fast trading and quick profit are the usual objectives. Nor is this surprising in an economic environment in which much business tends to be petty and transient, and in which even big business depends for its profits more on the vagaries of international commodity fluctuations than on the slow improvement of the domestic market.

Yet another difference in social attitudes is to be found in that critically important sector, government officialdom. In the West, by and large, we associate the idea of government personnel with that of a civil service bureaucracy.

[11] *Ibid.*, p. 81.

And this is particularly true as we go into the larger agencies and higher branches of government. We expect to find there, not only an incorruptible judiciary and legislature, but an impersonal hierarchy of technical experts.

Quite different traditional attitudes characterize the majority of the underdeveloped lands. Here "squeeze," nepotism, petty and large-scale graft are taken as the norm for government operation rather than as the occasional exception. In Latin America, for example, as Albert Hirschman writes, "Frequently the state is compared to the organized bandits of the backlands exacting their tribute and leading a purely parasitic existence. The idea that economic development takes place in spite of, rather than because of, state action is well expressed in the Brazilian saying, 'Our country grows by night when the politicians sleep.' " [12]

To be sure, there is always a danger that generalizations such as these will distort a would-be portrait into a caricature. It need hardly be said that in most underdeveloped lands there exist some modern farmers, some skilled and disciplined workers, some highly efficient business executives and dedicated government officials. Yet the existence of these "Western" types is more apt to be the exception than the rule. One need examine only the history of one of the most advanced underdeveloped nations, such as Mexico, to encounter in living reality the social types we have described: inert peasants, undisciplined workers, gouging businessmen, and rapacious government officials.[*]

[12] *Latin American Issues* (New York, Twentieth Century Fund, 1961), p. 24.
[*] Some of these stereotypes take on added reality in that extraordinary document of Mexican life, *The Children of Sanchez,* by Oscar Lewis (New York, Random House, 1961). See also his *Five Families* (New York, Basic Books Inc., 1959).

Let us complete this survey of social types by pointing up two conclusions. The first is that we find ourselves, in the typical underdeveloped country, facing a structure of social stratification unlike any we know from our own historic experience. Not only is the social distance between classes incomparably greater than that which separates upper and lower classes in the West, but class consciousness is also far more pronounced. An awareness of enormous social differences, a feeling of "belonging" to a certain class and of having little or nothing in common with a higher or lower class, is very much a part of the underdeveloped scene, whether in India, in Latin America, in the Near East, or in Africa.

This does not mean a *militant* class consciousness. On the contrary, the prevalent attitude of both upper and lower ends of the social spectrum is one of acquiescence in the existing social stratification. But the existence of huge differentials within society has its important political consequences nonetheless. It implies—perhaps it necessitates —a traditional structure of power based upon the maintenance of the profound inertia of the lower classes. When the gulf which divides rich and poor is as impassable as that of a backward nation, we cannot expect to find on the part of the favored classes an interest in change, in ferment, in "progress." The *anciens régimes* of the poor nations—many of which are still current *régimes*—find their natural self-interest in the preservation of accepted ways, or, at most, in the most cautious introduction of new social outlooks and opportunities.

Second, it is apparent these social types and social structures do not tend to produce economic systems which are capital-creating. Peasants do not and cannot create for

51

themselves large surpluses which can be reapplied to their lands. A ragged and casual labor force does not generate so much as a trickle of savings. The middle classes are weak and small. And most important, while the upper classes do amass a very considerable flow of investable profits, they do not find their traditional interests directed toward investing those profits into the channels required for development.

Thus the societies of underdevelopment suffer from an economic inertia which springs in the final analysis from social institutions and attitudes. In place of the culture of striving so characteristic of the West, a culture of acceptance weakens the determination and action necessary for the Great Ascent. While only someone unacquainted with the never-ending labors of the backward lands could claim that their populations "do not work," nonetheless it is true that work does not carry the freight of hope, and therefore the psychological attraction, of the West. Hopelessness breeds dispiritedness; resignation feeds upon and justifies itself. An enormous gulf of motives as well as of institutions and productive capabilities separates the poor lands from the rich. "The underdeveloped countries are not simply less prosperous models of the wealthy nations," said a lecturer at the University College of Ghana recently. "There are embedded in their structure factors which make for inertia and even retrogression." [13]

The great transformation

All these ways of thought and behavior are capable of change. The traditional suspiciousness of the peasant can

[13] Inaugural Lecture, Dr. Adam Curle, February 15, 1961.

give way—as it did in postfeudal Europe—to a "commercial" approach to farming. A raw labor force can become disciplined into the industrial army of a modern state. Merchants can become businessmen; government sinecurists can turn into civil servants. But a focus on the obstacles raised by social attitudes begins to make us aware of how inadequate a description of the Great Ascent is contained in the words "economic development."

For *economic* development—that is, the deepening flow of incomes and the widening flow of production—is itself dependent on the presence of an "economic" population: of production-minded farmers, industrial workers, enterprising factory managers, helpful government officials. So long as these do not exist, economic development cannot commence on a broad base.

True, a few showplaces of industrialism can be erected; steel mills can rise next to paddy fields; even a small industrial complex can take shape. Yet, as is shown by the juxtaposition of a prosperous São Paulo with a desperate Brazilian northeast, or the existence of an immense mining operation in Katanga with a totally underdeveloped hinterland, or a heavily industrialized Damodar Valley within sight of primitive Indian hillsmen, the mere laying-in of a core of capital equipment, indispensable as that is for further economic expansion, does not yet catalyze a tradition-bound society into a modern one. For that catalysis to take place, nothing short of a pervasive social transformation will suffice: a wholesale metamorphosis of habits, a wrenching reorientation of values concerning time, status, money, work; an unweaving and reweaving of the fabric of daily existence itself. And as we have seen, for such a social reorientation to take place, a precondition must be the replacement of regimes based on a perpetuation of the *status quo* by regimes audacious enough to unleash social change.

We shall revert to this crucial problem of political catalysis at a later point. Here let us emphasize only the fact that in any society such a transformation is a profoundly dislocating experience. We have but to think of the painful struggles which accompanied the evolution of our Western "modern" society out of its feudal matrix to remind ourselves that the habits of thought and action acquired over generations are not lightly shed. The process takes time—even in the West, after several centuries, when we look at the peasants of southern Italy, or the government of Spain, it is clearly not yet complete. How long it may take in the underdeveloped nations cannot be foretold. What is certain is that economic development, in the sense of a broadly based and shared upward climb, must wait on the establishment of social change on the grand scale.

The quicksand of population growth

But we have not yet completed our survey of the endemic problems of the underdeveloped lands. There still remains to be considered the hurdle which, by virtue of its immediate impact, may well pose the most formidable of all the barriers to progress. This is the overwhelming problem of population growth.

No one who looks for very long into the question of population growth in the underdeveloped areas can refrain

from a feeling of impending catastrophe. A few figures
are all that are needed to make the point.

Let us begin with our southern neighbor, Mexico. Today
Mexico has a population equal to that of New York, Penn-
sylvania, New Jersey, and Connecticut—36 million in all.
Forty years from now, if Mexico's present rate of population increase continues, it will have 123 million people—as
many as the present population of the four states above, *plus*
the rest of New England, *plus* the entire South Atlantic
seaboard, *plus* the entire West Coast, *plus* Ohio, Indiana,
Illinois, Michigan, and Wisconsin. Or take the Carib-
bean and the Central American area. Today that relatively
small area has a population of 66 million. In forty years,
at its present rate of growth, its population will outnumber
by thirty million the entire population of the United States
today. By that year South America, now 20 percent less
populous than we, is likely to be 200 percent larger than
our present population. At current rates of increase, India
will then number a billion souls, China 1.5 billion.

It is possible that these cancerous rates of growth will
decelerate, although no such trend is as yet evident. If
they do not, their impending impact on development is
all too obvious. Take, for instance, the case of the Aswan
High Dam in Egypt—one of the most colossal engineering
undertakings in any underdeveloped nation. The dam,
which will be as high as a thirty-story building and three
miles long, will make available approximately two million
acres of new land for crops. It will generate three times
the total amount of electricity now produced in Egypt.
Its over-all impact on increased agricultural production
may run as high as 45 percent. Meanwhile, however, that

figure happens to be the percentage by which Egyptian population is estimated to rise in the ten-year period during which the dam will be under construction. Hence, despite the long-term gain in power, the near-term effect in raising per-capita living standards will be zero. So far as immediate results are concerned, the entire gigantic enterprise will only succeed in preventing the Egyptian economy from suffocating under its proliferating human mass.

And the same bleak outlook is found on the other continents. Calculations show that Asia, merely to *maintain* her present low level of living standards, must *increase* her aggregate product by 60 percent between now and 1975, and by an additional 75 percent between 1975 and 2000. Thus the bulk of any gains from increased productivity is used up merely in sustaining the ever-threatened level of subsistence.

We have already seen one result of the relentless proliferation of people in the fragmentation of landholdings. But the problem soon goes beyond mere fragmentation. In India, Eugene Black tells us, already a population equivalent to that of all Great Britain has been squeezed out of *any* landholding whatsoever—even though they still dwell in rural areas. Hence population pressure generates massive and widespread rural poverty, and a push from the countryside into the already teeming and overcrowded cities. In Java, where population density has reached the fantastic figure of 1,100 per square mile (compare American population density of 50.4 people per square mile), five hundred families a day move into Jakarta from the surrounding fields. Two hundred and fifty families a day move into Bangkok and Rangoon. The crowd of beggars, street-livers, and scavengers grows.

It is an ironic commentary that the population explosion is a fairly recent phenomenon, and attributable, largely, to the incursion of Western medicine and public health into the underdeveloped areas. Prior to World War II, the poorer countries were generally marked by high birth rates, but their population increase was held in check by comparable death rates. Since then, the birth rates have continued high, but the death rates have plunged dramatically—and with unexpectedly tragic consequences. In Ceylon, for example, the death rate dropped 30 percent in the single year 1946 following the adoption of malaria control and other health measures. In Taiwan, in Malaya, in vast areas of Africa and the Near East, comparable extensions in the span of life—and in the ensuing bulge of population—have taken place. And the explosion of populations is not over. In tropical Africa today infant mortality runs between 200 and 800 per thousand, and averages 300 to 500 per thousand. There is an enormous source of future population growth as these ghastly rates begin to fall (as they will) toward the American infant death rate of twenty-six per thousand.

Will this self-defeating pattern of high birth rates continue? This, too, is a matter to which we will return. But it is well to conclude our brief survey of the problem with the somber words of Eugene Black: "Unless population growth can be restrained, we may have to abandon for this generation our hopes for economic progress in the crowded lands of Asia and the Middle East."

Vicious circles

And so we complete our initial survey of the underdeveloped countries. The problems we have itemized in the last few pages are, of course, by no means a complete catalogue of the common handicaps of underdevelopment. Moreover, as we have already noted, we must not suppose that all underdeveloped nations suffer from these handicaps in precisely the same way. In each the mix of the ingredients differs; in each there may be additional factors no less deeply rooted or intransigent: caste barriers in India, a disdain for work among the men of certain tribes of Africa, uneconomic notions of "fairness" in Java.

And then we have not even mentioned as yet the problems of health or of ignorance—problems which in every underdeveloped land produce a sucking undertow against the force of development. Take, for instance, malaria. More than 100 million people are today threatened by malaria; in a country like India, a fifth or more of the population may be unable to work for some period of each year because it is down with malarial fever. In Afghanistan, wide sections of arable lands around Kunduz are uncultivated for the same reason; the Afghan saying is, "If you want to die, go to Kunduz." In Mexico, malaria costs the nation an estimated $175 million a year in crops lost because their cultivators are unable to tend them.

Malaria is, of course, only one part of the health problem which undermines economic development. Yaws, a horrible, erosive disease which can be totally cured by

58

five cents' worth of penicillin, until recently afflicted an estimated fifty million people a year. TB, "the quiet killer," has taken five million victims a year; leprosy claims up to twelve million sufferers; trachoma, the blinder, impairs the eyesight of some 400 million. All of these diseases are the target of WHO and UNICEF programs; and all of them have begun to yield before the first international medical crusade in history, but they still constitute a major stumbling block to development: in Africa, for instance, malaria kills off about 12 percent of all Africans before they reach maturity. In other words, over fifteen million Africans live only long enough to consume their share of the continent's meager output, but not long enough to contribute to it.

Sickness is not the only developmental block to which we have paid inadequate attention. There is hunger, which can be equally crippling to human energy; ignorance, which can serve even more tellingly to hinder development; isolation—roadless villages, totally insulated communities—which can underlie ignorance. The list could be many times lengthened.

This complex multi-causality of underdevelopment can be summarized in the often-used expression "vicious circles." It is not "just" a lack of capital, or "just" backward ways, or "just" a population problem, or even "just" a political problem, which weighs upon the poorer nations. It is a combination of all of these, each aggravating the other. The troubles of underdevelopment feed upon themselves; one cannot easily attack one of the shackles of underdevelopment without contending with them all.

These are the hard—the brutally hard—difficulties of

underdevelopment. An interlocking of evil conditions, a self-generating tendency toward defeat, are the overwhelming realities which greet anyone who looks into the conditions of existence of most of mankind today and the prospects which stare it in the face for tomorrow. Nothing is gained by minimizing this grim condition. It is only by coming to grips with the problem in its full magnitude that we can begin to formulate plans adequate to deal with it.

But it is still too soon to turn to remedies. For we have not yet discussed what is perhaps the most important common attribute of the underdeveloped nations. This is their new-found dedication to development itself. How this came to be, and in what way it will bear upon the future, are the matters to which we must next turn.

THE
GREAT
RESOLVE

IV

A fact of which we can easily lose sight in studying economic development is how ancient is the condition with which it contends. If poverty is the basic measuring rod, then surely underdevelopment is as ancient as recorded civilization. Hobbes' famous characterization of life as "poor, nasty, brutish and short" is a fair generalization of the typical biography since time immemorial.

And yet underdevelopment as a "problem" is very recent. For into the traditional situation of the backward areas have come two radically new ingredients. The first is the availability of an industrial technology, now concentrated among a few advanced nations, which is capable of performing hitherto unimaginable feats of economic hydraulics. The second is an awakening, on the part of the peoples of the underdeveloped areas, to the remediable nature of their human condition. Together these forces have combined in a great resolve which underlies the development revolution. It is a commentary of some sort on human history that this resolve has only now emerged as a program for mankind, and that even now the very idea is regarded by some members of the favored quarter of humanity as premature.

Ideally, perhaps, a history of this idea should take as its starting point the web of causes by which that favored quarter began its own economic development in Europe in the sixteenth and seventeenth centuries. But that would take us beyond the confines of this small study. Instead, we can take as our point of departure the situation as it existed in the late nineteenth century, when the seeds of the present great resolve were first planted.

If we then spread out a map of the world in, say, 1900, we find a very interesting picture. Economically, the map looks much the same as it does today. But politically it is very different. From Egypt to the Union of South Africa, the continent of Africa was almost entirely white European real estate. Southeast Asia was dominated by Britain and Holland. China was a moribund society milked by various European concessionaire groups. Only South America appears as politically independent, and here, whatever the appearance, we do not have to look very deeply to discern the powerful influence of American, British, and European capital in its coffee and banana plantations, its meat-packing plants, its copper and tin mines, its chicle and sugar cane and sisal fields.

Thus what we see as the background for the present-day situation was the coexistence of two totally different, almost entirely separated, and yet dangerously interacting worlds. One was the dynamic, expansive, vigorous, self-assured world of capitalism in its heyday of imperialism. The other was the stagnant, passive, preindustrial world of the colonial or quasi-colonial nations and territories.

We need not here go into the complex history of imperialism and colonialism—a history which is only today drawing to its bitter end. But we must take note of the heritage of this history if we are to understand the course of economic development. Colonialism and imperialism are the schools in which most of the underdeveloped nations learned their lessons, and although the schooling was very different from colony to colony, a common distaste for their instructors is all too clearly apparent among all of the ex-students.

The initial impetus

It is not uncommon, when we review the long years of Western hegemony over the continents of the East and South, to highlight the ugliest side of that relationship. Ugly it often was, and ugly it continues to be in those areas, like Angola or the Rhodesias, where the nineteenth century continues into the twentieth.

But in the final appraisal, the impact of colonialism was far more than merely exploitative. For with the economic bridgeheads of the colonizing powers came the first massive injections of industrial capital into the underdeveloped areas. Roads, railroad trackage, docks, mine equipment, warehouses, cranes—all these were originally installed by the Western powers. To be sure, they formed more of an

63

extension of the colonizer's economy than an integral part of the colony's; they often remained as little islands of industrial activity, largely ruled by an isolated Western management clique, in a sea of unchanged peasant life. Nonetheless they brought the first major accretions of industrial wealth without which the underdeveloped economies would today be even more hopelessly retarded.

Equally important was a second import from the Western powers. This was the establishment of law and order which, in many cases, was more stable and more equitable than the native rule which it displaced. Admittedly, it was white man's law and white man's order—often discriminatory in its application and heedless of long-established local customs. Yet for many underdeveloped nations it was also a vital step toward a modern political administrative system.

But by far the most important positive effect of colonialism—albeit an unintended one—was its stimulation, in the minds of the colonial peoples themselves, of an awareness of their disfavored lot in life. For the handful of "natives" who went to England, Holland, France, and the United States to study, the philosophy and vitality of the West were an exciting discovery. To be sure, the philosophy was not meant for export, and when the young intellectuals went home to preach democracy, equality, liberty, and economic progress, their schoolmasters frequently rewarded them by placing them in jail. Withal, the lessons took, and the West must be credited with their instruction, if not with their implementation.

Thus the movement for economic development can be seen as the end-product of imperialism itself—the outgrowth of the diffusion of the cultural, social, and political background of the West into those areas in which an indigenous preparation for economic growth had not spontaneously appeared. However painful that interaction may have been, without it the impetus toward economic development might still be lacking in the underdeveloped world.

Lopsided development

If, however, one consequence of contact with the West was to inaugurate the initial impetus toward development, a less happy consequence was to start development off on a lopsided course.

For in the eyes of the imperialist nations, the underdeveloped regions were essentially seen as immense supply depots for the cheap production of raw materials from which their industrial economies could profit. Accordingly, the economies of the underdeveloped areas were often deformed into mere subsidiaries of their Western masters. Malaya became a rubber plantation, Rhodesia a copper mine, Ceylon a huge tea plantation, Arabia an oil field. Without doubt, the existing resources of the regions and the natural advantages of an international division of labor encouraged this tendency. But the direction of economic development was determined by their Western economic overlords, rather than by the peoples of the colonial lands, and the potential benefits of specialized industrial production failed to materialize for the underlying population.

Even in Latin America, which was relatively free of direct foreign manipulation, this one-sided growth resulted in severely misshapen economies. Today, for instance, Venezuela is dependent for 92 percent of its exports on oil, Colombia for 77 percent of its foreign earnings on coffee, Chile for 66 percent of its exports on copper, Bolivia for 62 percent of its exports on tin, Honduras for over 45 percent of its exports on bananas.

Hence another part of the imperialist heritage was the "one-crop" economy—an economy dangerously vulnerable to the vagaries of the international commodity markets. As a result, the underdeveloped world emerges from the age of imperialism with economies which are as badly overbuilt in some areas as they are underbuilt in others. Rather than being launched to weather all storms, they are setting sail in economic vessels which may easily be capsized by the winds of trade.

Understandably, this deforming result of past economic contacts strongly affects the attitude of the developing nations toward economic relationships with the West today. Despite the fact that the new nations, with the exception of those in the communist orbit, realize their desperate need for Western aid, Western advisers, Western loans and investments, they also regard each fresh incursion of Western capital into their territories with a wary eye. They see a new threat of foreign domination over their economic lives, not by overt political hegemony but by the vote of a board of directors sitting in London or New York or Amsterdam.

Consequently, in most underdeveloped countries we find elaborate laws insisting on local control over corporate policy. We find, as well, a willingness, often born of necessity, to use foreign corporations as scapegoats for domestic difficulties. Along the same line, we discover an understandable temptation to nationalize foreign corporations, especially when these control critical utilities. Having paid for most of these installations several times over through the profits which they have siphoned out of the country, even moderate nationalist leaders are tempted to take them over, even if they must be paid for one last time.

Closely associated with this general economic xenophobia is another attitude also springing from the imperialist past. This is the hesitant attitude we find among the political leaders of the underdeveloped world toward capitalism itself. This is not to say that these leaders lean toward communism—of that, more later. It is rather an expression of the fact that the only capitalism with which they are profoundly acquainted is that of the late nineteenth and early twentieth centuries—the harsh capitalism which reached its zenith in the movement of imperialism itself. Not surprisingly, then, we find that "capitalism" is a word associated with an unsavory tradition of exploitation, and that "socialism" is the word which expresses their idealized hopes for the future.

Political and economic resentments

Perhaps even more important than the failure of the imperialist powers to build effective economies in the underdeveloped areas was their failure in another direction—an inability to achieve political and psychological relationships of mutual respect with their colonial subjects. The terrible color line which relegated "the natives" to a position of irremediable inferiority, the galling political domination, the attitude of the Western powers to the poverty for which they may not have been responsible but toward which they remained largely indifferent—all this has left in the underdeveloped world a deep and only slowly healing wound.

One result of this political and psychological rejection is that the underdeveloped world has turned toward nationalism with all the fierce sentiments of a people who have long been denied their identity and status. The psychological appeal of nationalism is still far from well understood, but of its capacity to marshal the most powerful emotive response there is no doubt. The sense of being Indian or Nigerian or Lebanese or Brazilian runs even deeper and more passionately, at least in the politically minded classes, than do similar sentiments in the West, and this nationalistic orientation is given additional fervor by grounding itself in the yet more primitive and powerful awareness of being members of disprivileged races.

As we shall see, such nationalistic and racist attitudes may have their "functional" value in providing a rallying ground—perhaps the only rallying ground—for nations which must expose their populations to the arduous and disorienting experience of development. But at the leadership level, these attitudes of supernationalism have another meaning as well. They express, however irrationally, the hypersensitivity of proud men and women who smart under the arrogance of the white color mentality. Whereas it would be a misleading simplification to place a sense of racial injustice at the center of the political currents of the developing countries, it would be equally foolish to forget the powerful sentiments which are there ready to be mobilized against the white-supremacist West and in particular against the most primitive of Western countries in this regard, which is the United States.

The focus of aspiration

It is only by setting economic development into this embittered context that we can gain perspective on the great movement which is now commencing. For the final understanding with which we must conclude this capsule of historic background is that the great resolve has indeed been made. The bonds of colonialism and imperialism have been sundered or are now being cast off. A wave of nationalist feeling, of vividly felt national and racial identity and importance, has swept over the great continents which for so long formed only a passive background for Western history.

It would be foolish to romanticize this sweep of newly aroused ideas and expectations. For the great masses of the peasantry and city poor, the awakening of the mid-twentieth century is still only vaguely experienced. If it expresses itself at all, it is likely to find its voice in the intense nationalism we have just mentioned as a characteristic of a developing nation. The immediate carriers of the torch for *economic* development, as contrasted with political independence, are apt to be not so much the poorest classes as a leadership elite—a small but powerful group of political leaders, army officers, intellectuals. Here is where the drive for development is greatest, for these leaders understand, in a larger frame of reference than their illiterate or semiliterate countrymen, that only by a total economic severance with the past and an equally total economic effort for the future can the present lot of their countries be remedied. Hence we find that for these leaders, as Sir Robert Jackson has written: "Development has become the test of nationhood, the index of political success, the touchstone of acceptability into the modern community of nation states. In all the states moving out of colonial tutelage into sovereign independence it is *the* fundamental political issue." [1]

The point must be stressed, for many people, looking at the abysmally low starting point of development, reflecting on the pride and dignity of the shepherd, the simple peasant, or desert nomad, and foreseeing already the squalor and indignity to which they will be subject as mill hand and miner, cannot help asking: "Why go on with development? Why not stabilize, perhaps improve, the ways of the past?"

Generally the question is a sentimental one, for the pictured dignities of the past are either unrecapturable or dingy upon closer acquaintance. But there are more compelling reasons for acquiescing in economic development.

The first we have already noted. It is the fact that the incursion of Western medicine has broken an age-old balance of population and productivity, and precipitated a situation in which not stasis but deterioration is the terrible fate which stares nearly every backward country in the face. From the relentless, crushing increments of population there is no escape, short of plague and mass death, other than a swift ascent to a new level of industrial provisioning.

[1] *Foreign Affairs,* October, 1958, p. 57.

But there is a second reason as well. Out of the long apprenticeship of imperialist subjugation, out of the convulsive changes and sufferings of two world wars, out of the gradual infiltration of revolutionary ideas—the ideas of the French and American no less than of the Russian revolutions—an irreversible chemical change has taken place in the outlook of the hitherto ignored nations of the world. A desire for change, a disavowal of the past, a revulsion at the present, have transformed the basic human attitudes in the backward lands. And as these new sentiments find expression in new national governments, they seek their realization in economic development, with all its fearsome strains and stresses, but its still beckoning benefits and promises.

This choice, however much it may underestimate the trials of the transition, and however much it may overestimate the satisfactions of economic progress, is nonetheless an unanswerably valid one. It may very well be that in choosing the road to industrialization the underdeveloped lands are preparing for a period of distress and disorder far greater than any they have heretofore known. It is almost certain that industrialization will force upon leaders and underlying population alike trials and disappointments of such magnitude that the past, softened by distance, will often appear more attractive than the future, and the whole long march pointless and hopeless. And yet, given the realities of underdevelopment today and the overwhelming likelihood that under the population flood conditions can only worsen unless drastic remedies are tried, the decision is beyond possible dissent. For there is no possible alleviation for the hunger of the majority of the world, no possible replacement of its hovels, no manageable redress of its misery, short of a prolonged and profound economic reorganization of their lives.

Now the question is: Can the aspirations be fulfilled? Can the Great Ascent succeed?

THE
ENGINEERING OF
DEVELOPMENT

V

Heretofore we have concentrated our attention on the many factors, social, economic, and political, which go to make up the condition of backwardness. Our review has stressed the difficulties, the ingrained resistances, the psychological framework within which something called economic development must take place. So far, however, we have not discussed the mechanics of economic growth—which is to say, the way in which a poor country becomes richer. For despite everything that we have said (and will say again) in regard to the political and social preconditions for development, there is still an *economic* task whose nature we must understand if we are to gauge the chances of the Great Ascent.

And so we must set ourselves two questions to answer. First, is economic development possible? That is, given the starting point, the deficient productivity, the lack of capital, the population pressures—in short, all the *economic* variables in the development equation—is it possible to arrive at a sanguine economic forecast for output and incomes in the developing nations?

And second, whether development is possible or not, how does a nation try to mount its economic offensive? What are the economic forces which can be brought to bear, what are the needed shifts in and additions to the collective national effort? In a word, how does a nation pull itself up by its bootstraps?

The hidden potential

From what we have learned about the strictly economic aspect of underdevelopment we know already what the core process of economic expansion must be. It must consist of raising the low level of productivity which in every underdeveloped area constitutes the immediate economic cause of poverty. This low level of productivity, as we have seen, is largely traceable to the pervasive lack of capital in a backward nation. Hence if such a nation is to grow—if it is to increase its output of food, to expand its scale and variety of manufacturing—clearly its first economic task is to build up capital. The meager productive capacities of bare hands and bent backs must be supplemented by the enormous leverage of machines, power, transport, industrial equipment of every kind.

But how does a backward nation begin to accumulate the capital it so desperately needs? The answer is no different for a backward nation than for an advanced one. In every society, capital comes into being by saving. This does not necessarily mean putting money in a bank. It means saving in the "real" sense of the word, as the economist uses it. It means that a society must refrain from using all of its current energies and materials to satisfy its current wants, no matter how urgent these may be. Saving is the act by which a society releases some portion of its labor and material resources from the tasks of providing for the present so that both can be applied to building for the future. Again, as the economist would put it, saving means the freeing of labor and resources from consumption-goods production so that they may be applied to capital-goods production.

This release of productive effort directed to present consumption wants, in order to make room for effort directed at the future, does not present an overwhelming problem to a rich nation. But the problem is different in a poverty-stricken one. How can a country which is starving restrict its current life-sustaining activities? How can a nation, 80 percent of which is scrabbling on the land to feed itself, redirect its energies to building dams and roads, ditches and houses, railroad embankments and factories, which, however indispensable for the future, cannot be eaten today? The peasant painfully tilling his infinitesimal plot may be the living symbol of backwardness, but at least he brings forth the roots and rice to keep himself alive. If he were to build capital—to work on a dam or to dig a canal —who would feed him? Who could spare the surplus when there is no surplus?

In capsule this is the basic problem which most underdeveloped lands face, and on the surface it seems a hopeless one. Yet when we look more deeply into it, we find that the situation is not quite so self-defeating as it seems. For a large number of the peasants who till the soil are not just

feeding themselves. Rather, in so doing, they are also robbing their neighbors. In the majority of the underdeveloped areas, as we have seen, the crowding of peasants on the land has resulted in a diminution of agricultural productivity far below that of the advanced countries. In India, we will remember, a hectare of land produces only about one-third of the crop raised on a hectare in the United States. Hence the abundance of peasants working in the fields obscures the fact that *a smaller number of peasants, working the same fields, could raise a total output just as large—and maybe even larger.* One observer has written: "An experiment carried out near Cairo by the American College seems to suggest that the present output, or something closely approaching it, could be produced by about half the present rural population of Egypt."[1] Here is an extreme case, but it can be found to apply, to some degree, to nearly every underdeveloped land. It is widely estimated that between 15 and 30 percent of the agricultural population of most underdeveloped economies produce zero net output.[2] Whatever little crop they eke out is only won at the expense of someone else.

diminishing returns

The peasant problem

Now we begin to see an answer to the dilemma of the underdeveloped societies. There does exist, in nearly all of these societies, a disguised and hidden surplus of labor

---

[1] Charles Issawi, in Ragnar Nurkse. *Problems of Capital Formation in Underdeveloped Countries* (Oxford, Basil Blackwell, 1953), p. 35, footnote 2.

[2] *Ibid.*, p. 35.

which, if it were taken off the land, could be used to build capital. It is, to be sure, capital of a special and rather humble sort: capital characterized in the main by large projects which can be built by labor with very little equipment—roads, dams, railway embankments, simple types of buildings, irrigation ditches, sewers. However humble, these underpinnings of "social capital" are essential if a further structure of complex *industrial* capital—machines, materials-handling equipment, and the like—is to be securely anchored. Thus peasant labor released from uneconomic field work makes possible a crucially important first assault on the capital-shortage problem.

This does not mean, of course, that the rural population should be literally moved, en masse, to the cities where there is already a hideous lump of indigestible unemployment. It means, rather, that the inefficient scale of agriculture conceals a reservoir of both labor and the food to feed that labor. By reducing the number of tillers of the soil, a backward society can create a work force available to build roads and dams, while at the same time this transfer to capital building will not result in a diminution of agricultural output.*

This extraordinary feat of legerdemain lies at the heart of the economic side of development. It is not, however, just an *economic* feat. It is also intimately connected with another process which lies at the social core of develop-

* In sparsely settled lands we cannot apply the same strategy because there is no surplus population on the farm. Here we must *create* a surplus farming population by first raising agricultural productivity through better seeds, better technology, etc. This "created" surplus labor force can then be set to work building capital. The basic concept of this great transfer of resources is elegantly set forth in Ragnar Nurkse's classic *Problems of Capital Formation in Underdeveloped Countries.*

ment. This is land reform. For one cannot, after all, just go and "move people" in a living society. Deep-rooted legal and social institutions of landowning, of tenant-landlord and tenant-moneylender relationships must first be broken. Vested privileges in the old order must be overcome, often over the determined opposition of the landowning classes. Thus the mechanics of economic development immediately plunges us into the social and political problems of development.

But we can now also see something else of great importance. We can see that land reform is not just a matter of justice, of rescuing the peasant from the domination of a feudal landlord or a rapacious moneylender. It must also be a functional step, a step toward the formation of land units large enough to be farmed scientifically for high output. Land reform which merely breaks up large estates in order to parcel out tiny plots of soil is at best only a political palliative for the underdeveloped nation. Economically, it may even be a step backward toward fragmentation and inefficient subdivision.

However, let us revert to the immediate economic problem. We have seen how an underdeveloped society can increase its agricultural output and simultaneously "find" the labor resources it needs for development tasks. But where is the saving—the release of consumption goods—we talked about? This brings us to a second necessary step in our process of capital creation. When agricultural productivity has been enhanced by the creation of larger farms (or by improved techniques on existing farms), *part of the ensuing crop must be saved.*

In other words, whereas the peasant who remains on the soil will now be more productive, he cannot enjoy his enhanced productivity by eating up all his larger crop. Instead, the gain in individual output must be siphoned off the farm. The extra crop raised by the fortunate peasant must be saved by him, and shared with his formerly unproductive cousins, nephews, sons, and daughters who are now at work on capital-building projects.

We do not expect a hungry peasant to do this voluntarily. Rather, by taxation of various sorts, or by forced transfer, the government of an underdeveloped land must arrange for this essential redistribution of food.* *Thus in the early stages of a successful development program there is apt to be no visible rise in the peasant's food consumption, although there must be a rise in his food production.* Instead, what is apt to be visible is a more or less efficient, and sometimes harsh, mechanism for assuring that some portion of this newly added productivity is "saved"—that is, not consumed on the farm, but made available to support the capital-building worker. That is why we must be very careful in appraising a development program not to measure the success of the program by individual peasant living standards. For a long time, these may have to remain static—possibly until the new capital projects begin to pay off.

What we have just outlined is not, let us repeat, a for-

* Nurkse makes a sage comment in this regard. Speaking of the use of collective farms in Russia he writes: "The word 'collective' has here a double meaning. The collective farm is not only a form of collective organization; it is above all an *instrument of collection.*" *Op. cit.,* p. 43 (italics added).

mula for immediate action. In many underdeveloped lands, as we have seen, the countryside already crawls with unemployment, and to create a large and efficient farming operation overnight would create an intolerable social situation. Nor should we believe that the creation of such a modern agricultural sector can, in fact, be achieved overnight. Peasants, no matter how impoverished their condition, do not acquiesce gladly in radical rearrangements of traditional ways, nor do they relinquish without protest their tiny properties or their traditional connection with the soil. In the communist countries the collectivization of peasant holdings has everywhere been bitterly opposed. In nations as different as Cuba, China, Poland and Yugoslavia, zealous attempts to "reform" peasant attitudes and institutions have met with determined resistance, even to the point of sabotage. Nor have milder methods, such as the formation of cooperatives in India, met with much success in the face of inadequate educational backgrounds and technical experience.

Thus the social changes required to bring about a substantially improved condition of agriculture are likely to present severe problems to development-minded governments, authoritarian or democratic. Yet from the logic of the process there is no escape. In nearly every backward land, agricultural productivity *must* be enhanced if development is to take place, not alone to provide growing populations with food, but to create a labor supply for the formation of capital. Hence an amalgamation of small farming units into large ones, and a displacement of a considerable portion of the peasantry from the land, is a necessity for almost every developing country, no matter how painful the procedure.* The rate at which this can be accomplished, however, is apt to be slow. At best, we can envisage the process as a long-term transformation which extends over many years. It shows us, nonetheless, that a basic mechanism of development is the enforcement of a huge internal migration from agricultural pursuits, where labor is wasted, to industrial and other pursuits, where it can yield a net contribution to the nation's progress.

Industrialization

We have seen how a backward society has the hidden potential to build social capital. But capital-building is not just a matter of freeing men and food. Peasant labor may construct roads, but it cannot with its bare hands build the trucks to run over them. It may throw up dams, but it cannot fashion the generators and power lines that are needed if a dam is to produce energy. In other words, what is required to engineer the Great Ascent is not just a pool of labor. It is also a vast array of *industrial* equipment, which is the integral core of growth for all modern economies.

Sooner or later every developing region, if it is to carry its material advancement beyond the level of a fairly efficient agricultural economy, must build such a structure of industrial equipment—a structure of machine tools and

---

* In the West, the absence of the extreme population pressure characteristic of the underdeveloped lands made this rationalization of agriculture a less pressing precondition of development. Nonetheless, a rationalization process took place in many parts of Europe, especially in Northern Germany and England. England's early economic impetus was much facilitated by the enclosures which, by the mid-nineteenth century, had transferred half the arable land from smallholders to large commercial estates.

lathes, of specialized machinery of all sorts.* But there is a new difficulty here. For unlike the case of dams and irrigation ditches and basic housing, this new industrial capital itself requires prior capital. Roads and dams may be built, at least up to a point, by the sheer application of human labor working with the most primitive equipment. But lathes and looms, power shovels and machine shops cannot. The machines and equipment needed must themselves be made by machines and equipment. Thus there is a kind of endless circle here into which an underdeveloped country cannot break.

In fact, of course, it is not a circle but a spiral, for in the dim past the first machines were fashioned by primitive hand methods. If the underdeveloped countries had time, they could build an industrial capital sector much as the West originally did, by the slow process of accretion from handicraft. But time is what lacks above all in the race for development. Hence if industrial capital is to be added to the huge "public works" of social capital, the underdeveloped lands must find a way of bringing it into being in very rapid order.

What is that way? In part this critical equipment can be built within the developing country from its own manufacturing facilities, for only the most primitive regions have *no* machine shops or industrial capacity. But this is, at the very best, only a small part of the total industrial equip-

* This is not to say that every small nation-state of the moment, from Upper Volta to Viet Nam, can legitimately aspire to become a Switzerland or a West Germany. The point rather is that massive industrial centers must be built up within the great geographic regions of Asia, South America and Africa if these entire areas are to escape from their present agricultural servitude.

ment required. Many kinds of tools and apparatus are simply beyond the technical abilities of even the most advanced underdeveloped regions. And no underdeveloped country has even remotely the capacity to produce the over-all volume of industrial capital needed to sustain a rapid upward climb.

Hence the general answer to the problem cannot lie within the underdeveloped economies themselves. Instead, in the first stages of industrialization, before the nucleus of a machine-building sector has been laid down, the necessary germinal core of industrial capital must be obtained from abroad. Some may be purchased by the underdeveloped country in exchange for that part of its output which it has saved—i.e., not consumed—and shipped abroad as exports of raw materials or handicrafts. Some may be received as the result of private investment by Western corporations or individuals. And some may be had as "foreign aid"—that is, as gifts or loans from the advanced nations.

Thus for the first time we touch on the vital problem of the relationship of an underdeveloped nation to its more developed world neighbors, a matter to which we shall shortly return. But it is worth a moment's thought to place this relationship in proper perspective. Clearly, the pace of *industrialization* will depend heavily (although not exclusively) on capital goods obtained from abroad, whether by trade, investment, or aid. Yet it is also important to see that industrialization is itself only a stage in the over-all process of development. An industrial sector built before there is a supporting base of social capital, or before there has taken place a degree of agricultural reform, or before there has become visible some change in social attitudes, is likely to result only in an industrial enclave coexisting with a nondeveloped peasant society. Here are, in fact, the Damodar Valleys of India and the Union Minières of Katanga. For an industrial sector to take root, for it to exert a widespread economic and social influence throughout society, it will not suffice merely to bring in the machinery and equipment of industrialization. These must rather be planted in soil which has been at least partially prepared to receive them. Industrialization thus appears as the capstone of a successful development effort. And by the same token, the sheer growth of industrial output, without reference to agricultural output or to much less easily measurable skills and attitudes, is an inadequate index of the progress of the Great Ascent itself.

An over-all view: the take-off

Perhaps it is time to bring our investigations into focus. Hence let us assume, for the moment, that an underdeveloped economy has begun to change its agriculture, begun the slow metamorphosis of social habitudes, and succeeded in obtaining a flow of industrial capital from its own exports, from private investments, and from international aid. Can we then predict whether such a nation can commence a steady economic expansion which in time will bring it out of poverty and into the first stages of a modest well-being? Can we determine if it will generate capital at a fast enough rate to bring it, in W. W. Rostow's well-known phrase, to the point of "take-off"—that is, to the point at which its additions to capital make possible a *self-sustaining* increase in production?

An economist cannot answer this question for any particular country in the abstract. But he can isolate the main terms in the development formula which allow us to see how the different variables in the economic development process interact. They are three:

1. *The rate of investment which an underdeveloped nation can generate.*

As we know, this depends on the proportion of its current effort which it can devote to capital-creating activity, at first largely of a social, later of an industrial, kind. Clearly, the higher the saving—provided, of course, that it goes into capital projects and is not merely hoarded—the more feasible does the "take-off" become. In addition, foreign aid, although not "generated" from within, can be counted as part of the investment of a developing nation.

2. *The productivity of the new capital.*

The saving which goes into new capital eventually results in higher output. But not all capital boosts output equally. A million-dollar steel mill, for example, may have a very different effect on output from a million-dollar housing project. We can see that the higher the productivity of capital, the sooner will take-off be possible. On the other hand, some "low pay-out" investment, such as schooling, is necessary in order to move ahead on "high pay-out" capital, such as a modern factory.

3. *Population growth.*

This is the negative factor in the equation. If growth is to become self-sustaining, the rise in output must proceed faster than the diluting effects of population expansion. Otherwise *per-capita* output may be static or falling, despite a seemingly large rate of growth.

Here is what might be called the "iron law" of economic growth.[3] So long as the amount of savings, coupled with the fruitfulness of that savings, result in a rise in output which is faster than the rise of population, cumulative economic growth will take place.* Each year an increment of output will be won over the year before, and this increment in turn will yield *its* increment in successive years. Even seemingly small annual gains can in this way pyramid in time to impressive amounts, just as a small sum left to compound at a low rate of interest will, over the years, grow to very large size.

On the other hand, if the amount of savings is so low, or the productivity of the capital projects in which it is invested so small, that increased output fails to match increased population, the result must be stagnation or even retrogression. And this absence of economic growth will continue until one or more of the variables in the equation is changed—until savings rise, or the productivity of investment increases, or the rate of population expansion falls.

Thus economic theory begins to clarify for us the logistics of the Great Ascent—or, for that matter, of growth in an advanced nation. It shows us the principal economic variables which determine the great equation of economic progress. It allows us to think about a problem of enormous complexity within a fairly clear-cut framework of relationships. And to revert to the two questions with which we introduced our excursion into the theory of development, our

[3] The term is that of Dr. H. W. Singer.

* If, e.g., savings are 10 percent of income and if productivity ratios are one-third—that is, if each dollar of investment yields 33 cents of additional output—then over-all growth will take place at 3.3 percent a year (10 percent times one-third). As long as the rate of population increase is less than 3.3 percent a year, per-capita incomes will rise.

analysis shows us not only that economic growth, starting from underdevelopment, is *possible,* but the mechanics by which it becomes possible.

Nonetheless caveats are called for. As we have been at some pains to indicate, development does not consist solely in, nor can it be solely measured by, quantitative output. At best a sheerly economic analysis of growth points to a necessary, but not a sufficient, condition of the Great Ascent; and in singling out the criterion of output, it tends to divert attention from the critical factors of social and political change.

In addition, an emphasis on the economic variables tends to make of growth itself a purely mechanical process. It assumes, rather than demonstrates, that such a thing as "sustained" growth in fact occurs once the magical point of "take-off" is reached on the development curve. Yet a number of economies—such as Argentina or Turkey —have "taken off," only to make forced landings; others— one thinks of France before the war—became airborne but never flew very high; still others, presumably in orbit, crashed—as did the United States in 1929. The variables, in other words, cannot be pushed to the critical threshold and then left to themselves; on the contrary, it may take nearly as much effort to keep growth going as to get it going.

Hence it is well to keep the iron law of economic growth in perspective. It is a useful tool of analysis, not a magic formula for success. But if we use it cautiously, it can help us appraise the chances for economic growth of the under-developed areas. Let us look into some of the issues it opens for us.

THE
SPEED OF
DEVELOPMENT

VI

Our economic formulation shows us *how* growth can take place. But how *fast* can it proceed? The answer depends on the numbers we can insert into our development formula. Perhaps we should begin by trying to ascertain what numbers are *now* in the formula.

Not surprisingly, we cannot do this with precision. In most of the underdeveloped world even the most elementary statistics of national economic performance are only sophisticated guesswork. The prevailing estimates for the rate of gross investment run from 5 percent of Gross National Product for areas such as Afghanistan to over 20 percent in a few nations like Venezuela (where, however, it is largely concentrated in the oil enclave). The average is probably below 10 percent. Capital productivity ratios are subject to even wider variation, but are generally as-

$$\frac{I}{Y} \cdot \frac{\delta Y}{I}$$

THE SPEED OF DEVELOPMENT

sumed to average around one-third. Thus over-all growth may average between 3 and 4 percent annually (10 percent times one-third)—running much higher in some areas and lower in others. Population growth, the negative factor, averages around 2 percent, again displaying much local variance.

These very rough figures cannot be applied to the performance or prospects for any individual country. But as a first approximation to the problem, they allow us, however crudely, to cast up a set of general accounts with which to judge the progress of the underdeveloped areas as a whole.

When we look at the positive side of our ledger sheet, we perceive an astonishing fact. Against all the obstacles to development that we have described, economic progress has in fact been taking place, and at a pace which by comparison with the past amazes us with its rapidity. Over the last decade the backward nations as a whole have increased their aggregate national outputs by about 40 percent—virtually as large a rate of increase as that of the United States over the same period.

But there is still the debit side of the ledger to be considered. For while the backward nations increased their over-all income by 40 percent, nearly three-quarters of the gain was washed out by population growth. A number of countries in Latin America have seen an actual *decline* in per-capita food production as population has raced ahead of output. In Africa and the Near East and Southeast Asia, the food situation is almost as discouraging. In India, for instance, total agricultural production has risen some 20-25 percent since 1950, a rate which has barely balanced the population increase. In industry, performance was better: steel output over the decade rose by about 25 percent, coal by about a third, cement by over 100 percent, electric power by nearly 150 percent, fertilizer output by about 900 percent. Despite these impressive figures, however, the industrial sector is still so small that its impact on total growth is limited. From 1950 to 1958 India's Gross National Product rose but 30 percent in real terms, or, at best, only 1.5 percent a year faster than population growth.[1]

When we translate these meager results into individual realities, the figures seem to shrink still further. *During the last decade, net growth amounted to no more than an average of one dollar per year per person.* That is to say, it was virtually unnoticeable.

Take the example of India again. In our first view of underdevelopment we noted that one person in every 250 in India now owned a radio. This is an improvement of almost 100 percent over the situation in 1955. But what is an impressive rate of advance along the statistical curve is a rate of improvement of zero for the overwhelming majority of Indians. So too with bicycles. There are now 50 percent more bicycles per capita in India than four years ago. And still but one person in four hundred owns a bicycle.

With variations from country to country, this general result could be reproduced virtually everywhere over the map of underdevelopment. While a few nations, like Mexico, have mounted truly extraordinary increases in indus-

[1] Wilfred Malenbaum, "India and China: Contrasts in Development," *American Economic Review,* June, 1959, pp. 287-296.

trial output, many more nations look to India's modest record with envy. This is not to say that seeds for the future have not been sown or that remarkable strides have not been made. Undoubtedly the Great Ascent has begun to mount. What is disheartening is the agonizing slowness of its pace. In important areas of the world, such as Africa or the Near East, economic development over the past decade has amounted to little more than a holding operation, a precarious shoring-up of the rising tide of population. In India, the upshot of an unprecedented effort has been no more than to inch the economy forward. Even in the most hopeful regions, such as South America, nothing resembling "self-sustaining" growth has been achieved in the majority of nations.

Can the Ascent move faster? The answer, in the first instance, depends on whether new values can be substituted for old ones in the development equation. Let us look at the prospects for improving each of the factors critical for economic growth.

Population control

It is obvious that one great stumbling block to a quickened pace of development is the population problem. Hence one frequently hears that the underdeveloped countries should bend their first attention to curbing this self-destructive trend. Or one hears that the United States should make birth control a condition for the granting of aid.

There is no question that an effective control over population growth would be a tremendous contribution to development. Unfortunately, it is much easier to recommend than to institute. We forget that in many parts of the underdeveloped world children are a symbol of manliness, of prestige, to men who have no other source of status, no other thing which is theirs. We forget that children are also sources of domestic and field labor for families who have neither appliances nor farm equipment. We forget that children constitute the only "social security" in countries where childless old age can mean utter destitution.

Hence it is not so easy—nor even, in the individual instance, so humane—to urge the peasant or the city laborer to have fewer offspring. You may tell him that if everyone limits his family, all families will be better off, but the peasant and the laborer cannot act on such altruistic motives, any more than we can. You may tell him that having fewer children may help him rear them to adulthood, but he has no guarantee that if he has only two or three children an epidemic will not wipe out all his family instead of only half or three-quarters as before. You can tell him that birth control is simple and easy and safe, but he and his wife find it expensive, bothersome, difficult, mysterious. And finally— what else is there to do? As a doctor in Lucknow, India, recently told an interviewer, "Unless we offer the villagers and city masses some other kind of life than that of endless work, until we can substitute entertainment and recreation in the form of community life, radio, education, theater, etc., for their present entertainment after the day's work, the soaring birth figures will continue. Only uplifting the people and enlarging their cultural horizons will flatten out the curve."[2]

All these considerations begin to show us why one does

[2] S. Plastrik, "Return to India," *Dissent*, Spring, 1961, p. 170.

not simply "institute birth control," and thereby solve the problem at one fell swoop. The fact is that birth control programs are among the most difficult of social changes to inaugurate. In only one nation, Japan, has an effective birth control program been launched, and this program, which relies upon legalized abortion, has only legitimized a spontaneous form of population control. More significant, this spontaneous trend toward abortion itself *followed*, and did not lead, a substantial measure of economic improvement.

The last point is a highly important one. If we are to judge by the experience of the past, industrialization brings its own subtle forces to bear on the birth rate. The altered status of women, the economic disadvantages of children in an industrialized environment, the delayed age of marriage, and, not least, the expanded horizon of expectations, all exert pressures which seem to depress the natural birth rate: In Russia, for example, the rate fell from 36.3 per thousand in 1920 to 19.4 in 1955. Thus the great hope is that the cure for the population problem lies in the process of industrialization itself. The trouble is, however, that this takes time—a very long time. Meanwhile, the terrible rates of increase, especially in the years during which the death rate falls dramatically, themselves provide perhaps the most discouraging barrier to the achievement of rapid industrialization.

Is there no exit from this tragic impasse? Disasters of war or of mass disease provide one possible, if chilling, escape from the Malthusian trap. Emigration on a monumental scale offers another theoretical means of alleviation, at least for certain areas. More convenient techniques would undoubtedly help; conceivably an all-out campaign, carried on, not as now in India by means of persuasion, but with vigorously applied incentives and sanctions, might effectively stem the tide, albeit at considerable social and political cost.

At the moment, however, none of these dramatic developments is on the horizon and in all likelihood the situation will remain much as it is. To be sure, not every underdeveloped nation will feel this suffocating pressure, and for a few the problem is unimportant. One can take heart at an increasing willingness to recognize the problem in countries as different as Egypt and Chile. Between recognition and remedy, however, is a long step. In all probability, the trend of birth rates, at least for this generation, is likely to be a more or less fixed and tragic constant in the formula for development. Hence if development is to accelerate, we must look to the other terms in the equation—the terms which describe the increase in output rather than the increase in the number of consuming mouths. What can we safely predict about these?

Capital productivity

We will remember that there were two terms in the production side of the growth equation: one which stood for the supply of savings available for capital formation and the other which described the productivity of these savings when put to use. Let us begin by examining this last term: is it possible to boost the output of the underdeveloped nations significantly by increasing the productivity of their new investments?

It is curious that the critical question "By how much

94

does a given investment boost output?" is a relatively new one to economics. One reason is that the question is extremely complicated, and the answers, such as they are, by no means clear. It is common to assume that "on the average" a capital investment in an underdeveloped land will yield an increase in output of between a quarter and a half of its value—that is, that a million-dollar investment will result in increased annual production, year after year, of between $250,000 and $500,000. Yet these figures are extremely variable and by no means firm enough to allow us to use them for arithmetical games in projecting production possibilities. We cannot simply urge the underdeveloped nations to speed up their rate of growth by investing in "high pay-off" items, often because we do not ourselves know exactly which projects will pay off most highly. "We once had a spirited argument in the Bank," writes the President of the World Bank, "over whether a mining company that approached us for a loan to buy modern mining machinery would do more to increase productivity if instead it borrowed locally to build new houses for the miners." [3]

But if there is no simple prescription for maximizing the flow of additional output from a given sum of investment, one thing that can surely be done is to minimize the wastage of capital resources. Millions and even billions of dollars of savings have yielded a zero return over the past ten years, not because they have been hoarded or put into luxury goods, but because they have been spent for development projects that have failed to justify their expense.

[3] Black, *op. cit.*, p. 30.

We have already noted that many—perhaps most—of the backward nations begin their development efforts in a state of tragic ignorance about their own capacities. They do not know the extent or nature of their resources. They do not have accurate surveys of their land. They may very well not even know the size of their populations. Hence they are apt to launch development projects based more on guess and hope than on solid expectations for success.

This can easily lead to disaster. An instance is provided by the history of a British attempt to grow peanuts in Tanganyika after World War II. Plans were laid for a vast project. Over 1½ million acres of land were to be cleared at an estimated cost of £4 an acre, on which it was figured that a per-acre crop of seven hundred pounds of nuts could be raised. Two years later less than 200,000 acres had been cleared—at a cost of up to £20 an acre, and the yield was not seven hundred pounds per acre but only two hundred. In other words, the scheme provided peanuts at a cost of approximately 1700 percent greater than expectations.

What accounted for the failure? Largely it was a lack of adequate preparation. The soil had not been properly tested and turned into rock-like macadam under tractor weights. Rainfall patterns were inaccurately gauged. Transportation facilities were inadequate. A steady supply of skilled labor was hard to find.

The failure of the "groundnut scheme" was expensive for England; for an underdeveloped nation it might have been catastrophic. Hence preinvestment surveys—of resources, manpower, logistics—have increasingly been recognized as a prime necessity for effective growth.

By how much can the productivity of capital be raised

by the avoidance of misinvestment? Unquestionably, the prospects for a given investment project are greatly enhanced by careful preparatory work; the United Nations Special Fund, which does a great deal of preinvestment work, estimates that each dollar of resource survey yields $100 of sound investment possibility. On the other hand, the preparatory work is itself time-consuming—a year may have to be spent taking tidal measurements in order to determine how best to deal with the silting of an important harbor. And then, too, an emphasis on preinvestment inevitably encourages a piecemeal approach to development. It puts caution before courage; it tends to rule out the massive efforts which, however wasteful, may be the only way to achieve major results.

And even with the best-planned programs, there is a further stumbling block to development in the lack of skilled personnel to put effective capital projects into operation. When Libya, for instance, came into its independence in 1949, there were but five thousand Libyans who had had five years of any kind of schooling, and only fourteen university graduates in the country. In Africa as a whole, between 80 and 85 percent of the population is illiterate; fewer than 5 percent of the children who attend elementary school go on to secondary school; fewer than one percent go on into vocational institutes. In India, only half the childhood population goes to school—as is the general case in South America as well.

When we aggregate the lack of skills typical of every backward nation, the problem assumes staggering proportions. It has been estimated that Nigeria alone will require some twenty thousand top-level administrators, executives, technicians, and managers over the next ten years and at least double that number for middle-level jobs. On a world-wide scale this implies a need for at least 700,000 top-level trained personnel and twice as many qualified subordinates. Half this number would impose a hopeless task on the slim educational facilities of the poorer nations. In India, for example, only eighteen engineers are currently being trained per million of population, less than one-tenth the ratio of the United States.

In part, this deficiency can be made good by technical assistance from other nations or from the UN. The records of technical assistance programs abound with legitimate success stories—for instance, a Pakistan paper-mill project, stymied because there was not a single Pakistani trained to operate such an enterprise, was rescued by the provision of a UN-engaged Swiss paper-mill executive. But foreign assistance can scarcely begin to fill the deficit of skills which impedes development in most backward areas. By 1962 no more than ten thousand UN experts had been provided for the underdeveloped regions, and the UN Technical Assistance program is encountering severe difficulties in recruiting further experts. And despite the expanded scope of its program, as of 1962 the UN had been able to send only sixteen thousand nationals from the backward areas to technical training institutes at home and abroad.

Thus the outlook for raising the productivity factor in the development equation is not particularly bright, at least for the immediate future. As with the hope for an effective birth control technique, however, there is a *possi-*

bility for a more dramatic breakthrough. The development of new forms of technology, requiring little skill, adaptable to small-scale industry, and capable of high outputs, could significantly boost the productivity of a number of sectors in an underdeveloped country. Quite aside from the possibility of a small-scale, high-efficiency agriculture, one could imagine the growth of a modern, highly productive "cottage industry," capable of supplying many consumer items and even some industrial equipment.

As yet, however, such a technology does not exist, and small-scale industry, although a very useful part of the development effort, does not yield results which push up the over-all productivity factor in the growth equation. Nor does small-scale industry seem capable of providing a substitute for the vast capital agglomerations of heavy industry, as evidenced by the very disappointing results of the Chinese "back-yard" steel furnaces. Still less is small industry able to provide the great underpinnings of social capital which are a precondition for rapid industrial expansion.

For the moment, then, the chances for raising the productivity of capital rest mainly with preinvestment surveys and with technical assistance programs. Both of these are of the highest priority and will undoubtedly enhance the chances for success of innumerable individual projects. Finally, it is well to remember that even "wasted" investments may leave behind them their useful residues, not only of recoverable or reusable physical assets, but of invaluable experience. Given the magnitude of the total needs and lacks, however, it would be unwise to expect more than a modest contribution from these sources to the acceleration of the over-all development drive.

Raising the flow of savings

But we still have to consider the last of the terms in the development equation. This is the amount of additional savings which an underdeveloped nation can generate—the augmentation of the effort which it can devote to capital-building.

It is unlikely that large amounts of additional savings can be easily wrung from the great bulk of the population, the peasantry. In the majority of the underdeveloped nations today there is no savable surplus in the agricultural sector; indeed, as we have seen, one of the initial problems of development is to *create* such a surplus by rationalizing agriculture. A large increase in savings from the peasant sector depends, then, not only on the successful reorganization of landownership, but on the ability of a developing government to seize the peasant's surplus before it is consumed.*

It is equally difficult to squeeze savings from the small industrial working class. Indeed, one problem of development may be a premature acquiescence in high wages and welfare measures, in order to placate this strategic group. Such policies lead invariably to inflationary distress—as, for instance, in Argentina under Perón—but they are very difficult to undo. Note that in the Argentine elections of early 1962, the Peronista vote was so large that it led to the suppression of the electoral results by army coup. Sav-

---

* In point of fact, food intake is often so low that some of the surplus must be "invested" in higher per-capita food consumption levels to permit a sturdier work effort. Cf. H. Leibenstein, *Economic Backwardness and Economic Growth* (New York, John Wiley & Sons, 1957), pp. 64-65.

ings can be had from the industrial class, but, as with the peasant, they will have to be forced out by strict government control.

A much more propitious source of additional savings is to be found in the upper and middle classes. Here undoubtedly something can be done to tempt new savings into existence and to direct them toward industrial enterprise—the World Bank, for instance, has successfully presided over the flotation of a number of industrial stock issues which were sold in whole or part to members of the middle and upper classes who had never previously owned securities. Whether a truly substantial increase in savings can be obtained in this manner is perhaps less likely. If the desired increases run in the order of magnitude of 50 and 100 percent, once again they are more apt to result from measures to *force* saving than from attempts to induce it. Stringent curbs, for instance, may be imposed on luxury consumption and the subsequent unspent funds siphoned off by heavy income taxes or more-or-less compulsory loans.

Such measures again lead us to the inextricable political aspect of economic development. Tax reform, like land reform, is a perennial subject on the agenda of most underdeveloped nations, but both have remained for the most part only on the agenda. In similar fashion, the curtailment of luxury spending has met, at best, with limited results to date. Lavish personal expenditure continues to be the rule rather than the exception among the upper classes of every underdeveloped country. Nevertheless there can be no doubt that a *potential* for greatly increased saving exists. Provided that political resistance is overcome, there is

101

no prima-facie reason why domestic savings cannot rise considerably. At least the flow of savings, unlike the population problem and to a lesser degree the capital productivity problem, lies within the immediate control of the underdeveloped nations. It is certainly the most hopeful element in the growth equation.

We are not yet ready, however, to assemble the various elements of that equation. For we will remember that capital formation in an underdeveloped economy requires more than the release of domestic resources. It also depends critically on the transfer of *industrial* equipment from the advanced portions of the world. Hence we must now turn to the crucial problem of the relation of the underdeveloped lands to the advanced economies of the world.

Channels of trade

When we think of ways in which the advanced nations can help the less advanced, our thoughts tend to turn first in the direction of "aid"—that is, in the direction of the outright gifts or state-to-state loans which are almost a symbol of twentieth-century internationalism. But we are wrong to begin our consideration of the problem here. For the major economic contact between the advanced and the backward nations is not aid, but trade—not, that is, one-way transfers of goods, but two-way exchanges of goods brought about by the advantages accruing at each end of the transaction. Most of the vital additions to an underdeveloped nation's small stock of capital—most of its imported generators and lathes and girders and tractors—

have not been "given" to it. They have been bought and paid for with the proceeds of the goods—the coffee and tin, cocoa and rubber, iron ore and handicrafts—which industrialized nations need but cannot produce at home.

"We sometimes assume," writes Dr. Peter Kenen, "that the underdeveloped countries buy machinery, building materials, and other capital goods with borrowed money. But this is not so. Most low-income countries finance their imports for development with their income from exports. In 1957 only $13 out of every hundred spent by India on imports were borrowed abroad or given by foreign governments. Nearly $70 of each hundred were provided by Indian exports, and the balance came from accumulated reserves." [4]

In all, the underdeveloped countries earn about thirty to forty billion dollars a year from foreign trade. But not all that they buy with these earnings contributes to development. Much of the equipment they bring in is needed merely to *maintain* operations: steel rail, for example, must be imported not only to build new lines, but to replace worn-out trackage. In addition, an important fraction of an underdeveloped nation's earnings in foreign trade must be earmarked to pay interest on its foreign indebtedness. And in years of crop failure, exports must finance purchases of food.

Needless to say, there is no guarantee that a backward nation's export earnings will be wisely spent. There have been plenty of instances where dollars have ended up in Cadillacs and air-conditioners rather than in earth-moving

[4] *Giant Among Nations* (New York, Harcourt, Brace & Co., 1960), p. 98.

machinery or diesel engines. But as the urgency of development has grown more stringent, we find fewer and fewer luxuries being unloaded at tropical ports. The main problem for the backward countries is not one of squandering their foreign exchange; it is one of earning as much exchange as they can.

And this is not so simple. We have seen that most of the poorer nations are sellers of raw commodities—too often of only one commodity per country. This means that they are dependent for their foreign earnings on goods whose prices are notoriously unstable. Hence rather than being able to plan ahead for a fairly steady and reliable flow of earnings, they find their export receipts subject to wild and sometimes disastrous changes. The price of copper, for instance, rose by 42 percent from 1954 to 1955, then plunged by 34 percent in 1957 and by as much again in 1958. Coffee rose by 38 percent from 1953 to 1954, fell by 27 percent the next year and by 33 percent in 1958. Wool fell by over 50 percent from 1952 to 1958; cocoa by as much in the single year 1956.[5] Such fluctuations can deal staggering blows. It has been estimated, for instance, that for every penny by which copper falls on the New York market, the Chilean treasury loses four million dollars, and that each penny drop in the price of green coffee costs Latin America fifty million dollars. To be sure, as our instances show, these fluctuations can also give rise to tremendous windfalls. No small part of the over-all growth of the underdeveloped world during the first postwar decade was attributable to a

[5] Raymond Frost, *The Backward Society* (New York, St. Martin's Press, 1961), p. 225.

commodity boom—a fact which may hardly be reassuring for the long run but which must be given its due.

But there is yet another complication. Whereas raw commodities fluctuate both upward and downward in price, in recent years the manufactured wares for which they are exchanged have tended to fluctuate in only one direction—up. Thus the "terms of trade"—the actual *quid pro quo* of goods received against goods offered—have moved against the interests of the commodity exporter: he has given more and more raw material for less and less machinery.* The drop in coffee prices alone in the last ten years has cost the Latin-American countries over ten billion dollars. In 1957 and 1958 this adverse tendency assumed grotesque proportions when commodity prices fell badly, following a United States recession, and manufactured goods prices remained steady to higher. The result was that the poorer nations received some two billion dollars less in actual purchasing power, *which was more than all the "aid" they received that year.* In effect, the underdeveloped nations involuntarily subsidized the developed world.

What can be done about this? One thing, of course, is for the advanced nations to minimize their own economic fluctuations—or, as has been suggested, to arrange foreign aid in such a way as to compensate poor countries for unexpected export losses, should they occur. But there is also another remedy—and one which accords nicely with de-

---

* Over the long run this adverse movement of the terms of trade is undoubtedly compensated in part by qualitative improvements in industrial goods: the coffee exporter may have to give more sacks for a lathe, but the lathe is more efficient. This qualitative improvement is nonetheless apt to be swamped by the violence of year-to-year price changes.

velopment itself. This is for the underdeveloped nations to diversify their exports, to begin to send manufactured or semimanufactured goods into the world markets. On a limited scale this has, in fact, begun. Brazil is actually exporting autos, almost entirely of Brazilian origin and make, to Portugal; India may soon become a small exporter of steel.

But here we face a new hitch. Few of the advanced countries look with unalloyed delight upon the inflow of such goods into their economies. A number of nations, ourselves included, have already imposed restrictions on raw material imports, such as petroleum or zinc or lead, in order to protect domestic producers. In Europe, many countries further limit the market available to the underdeveloped nations by traditional sumptuary taxes on such goods as cocoa, tea, coffee, or tobacco. In 1961 President Frondizi of Argentina complained that his country lost $250 million of meat sales yearly because of the restrictions of the Common Market. This tendency to limit the import of raw commodities is apt to be intensified in the case of manufactured commodities. In America, for example, a flood of low-priced textiles from Hong Kong and Japan (a "flood" which has taken less than 10 percent of our market) has already provoked the threat of a union boycott of such goods, and a powerful labor-management drive upon Washington to secure "relief." The specter of "sweatshop goods" produced abroad has always frightened the American producer, and when those goods are produced by efficient machines as well as low-priced labor, perhaps rightly.

Thus the problem is far from simple. It has been suggested more than once that an effective international division of labor today might allow the advanced "industrial" nations to become the great food producers of the world and the backward "agricultural" nations the world's workshop. But it would be asking a good deal to expect an American garment worker, knocked out of his livelihood by the imports of low-priced shirts from India, to acquiesce philosophically in such a rearrangement of world production patterns. At the very least the displaced worker must be retrained, perhaps relocated, and certainly adequately sustained during his period of difficult adjustment.

Such adjustments, even on a relatively restricted scale, are costly and onerous. Yet they are not impossible. It may help us to undertake them if we realize that through aiding development by increased imports we also aid ourselves. For we are sellers as well as buyers in the international markets, and the amount we sell is directly affected by the level of development of our customers: compare the Netherlands, to which we export goods in the amount of $52 per inhabitant, with India, which buys 69¢ per inhabitant. Hence if we can lift the general level of well-being abroad, we are likely as well to lift our level of economic well-being at home. It has been estimated that if the underdeveloped world manages to raise its per-capita incomes by 2 percent a year over the next ten years, it will offer a market for U.S. products some fourteen billion dollars bigger than today. Over the decade ahead, that would mean an additional demand for the goods of all the advanced countries of nearly $150 billion.[6]

[6] Paul G. Hoffman, *One Hundred Countries* (Washington, D.C., 1960), p. 56.

There are signs that we are beginning to understand the primary role of trade in assisting the underdeveloped world on its way. U.S. Government circles are now fully aware of the importance of leveling out the commodity markets, and, significantly, the Committee for Economic Development, a leading business research group, has cautiously expressed sympathy with the aims and purposes of some commodity stabilization agreements[7]—a considerable change in business thinking. Even the most articulate opponents of "sweatshop imports" realize that we cannot arbitrarily deprive low-income countries of a chance to sell their goods and thus pay their own way toward development. An internationalist approach is beginning to permeate many quarters, here and in Europe. Sooner or later we will have to comprehend the fact that trade *is* aid, and that every limitation on the ability of the underdeveloped world to sell its products to the industrialized nations ultimately retards by just so much their eventual well-being.

The flow of private capital

The broad channels of trade are one main avenue by which the outside world can help development. A second extremely important source of economic leverage is the capital funds which the advanced nations invest in the underdeveloped lands.

Before World War II this flow of investment was, in fact, the main source of nontrade development capital for the then colonies or neglected nations. Enormous planta-

[7] *Cooperation for Progress in Latin America*, C.E.D. publication, 1961.

tions in the East Indies, huge mining operations in Latin America or the Congo, vast vegetable oil and fiber enterprises in Africa were founded, managed, and financed by capital supplied by the Western powers. It is a remarkable fact that England between 1900 and 1914 exported about 7 percent of its national income in the form of capital investments, largely to the underdeveloped regions.

If the Western world today exported a comparable percentage of its national income to establish new enterprises in these lands, the development problem might not look so formidable. But private investments have fallen to a fraction of prewar years. England, for example, invests only a little over one percent of its total income abroad, and only about a third of that in the poorer nations. The United States, in an average year, exports perhaps $500 to $1,000 million in private investment funds to the backward areas, or about one-tenth to one-fifth of one percent of its Gross National Product. Furthermore, of this sum, about 60 percent represents oil investments in North Africa, the Near East, and Latin America.

This precipitous decline in private investment is not difficult to explain. The old relationship of "mother country" and "colony" has been broken, breaking along with it the special productions and inducements which formerly attracted capital. The ravages of World War II at first impoverished many of the traditional lenders of Europe, and subsequently the European boom has diverted funds to their own capital-building needs. Not least, the troubled politics and strained economics of development have in turn constituted their own formidable barriers to a free inflow of foreign capital.

Nonetheless, although smaller, the flow of private investment funds continues. Since the mid-1950's roughly two billion dollars a year, more than half of it European, has traveled from the rich nations to the poor in the form of private loans or private investments. For the recipient nations this has brought a double benefit. On the one hand, much of this flow of capital materialized in the form of new capital assets—smelters or refineries or processing plants—which added directly to the productive or export capacities of the underdeveloped lands. Secondly, the majority of these new foreign enterprises paid taxes or royalties to the governments of the nations in which they were located and thus enhanced their financial strength. In Latin America, for example, approximately 20 percent of all taxes are paid by American companies.

Yet we must not overestimate the role which private investment has thus far played in promoting the development process. A very large part of private capital is invested abroad in the extractive industries—in mining and oil production. In fact, of all dividends and interest remitted by enterprises in the underdeveloped lands to their corporate owners in the industrialized nations, half comes from three major oil producers, Iran, Iraq, and Venezuela.

These extractive industry investments exert but a limited impact on the over-all economic way of life of the countries in which they are located. In Venezuela, for instance, expenditures for wages and materials do not exceed 20 percent of the value of oil exports; in the Middle East less than 5 percent of oil revenues are paid out as wages; in the Chilean or Bolivian or Northern Rhodesian mining enterprises, less than a third of receipts returns to the income stream as wages.[8] Thus in themselves the great extractive investments tend to form more or less self-contained entities within the surrounding economic countryside.

This is not to say that extractive investments are of no developmental significance. We have already mentioned that all underdeveloped governments share, in one form or another, in the fortunes of their mining and drilling enterprises, and this share can unquestionably be used to support development activity. Whether it will or not depends, as always, on the political complexion of the ruling regime. In Kuwait, for instance, a "modern" feudal regime uses a third of its oil royalties to create a "welfare" state, a third for general government purposes, and a third to enrich itself, with the result that the ruler of Kuwait is distinguished by the possession of the largest private account in the Bank of England. In Iraq, on the other hand, the bulk of oil royalties are expressly reserved for development projects, and in most Latin-American nations income from oil has made possible the financing of various development schemes.

It seems unlikely, however, that the extractive industries will play a galvanic development role in the future. More hopeful is the prospect that private manufacturing investment will provide a powerful stimulus to countries which have begun a rapid rate of economic growth. In the more advanced underdeveloped countries we find private investments beginning to fan out in variety and impact. In Mexico, for example, a writer for *Fortune* magazine has described a scene in which "Everywhere signs proclaim

[8] C. Rollins, "Minerals and Economic Growth," *Social Research*, Autumn, 1956, p. 259.

U. S. companies, General Motors, Singer, Goodrich, Studebaker, R.C.A., Eastman Kodak—only the corporate suffix 'S.A.' attests plainly that the locale is other than Rahway, N.J." [9] Private investment may thus become an extremely important agent in adding momentum to development once a vigorous climb has been commenced; let us not forget the critical role which British capital played in financing our own period of rapid economic development in the nineteenth century.

Realistically, however, it seems premature to expect a substantial widening of the flow of private investment in the immediate future. Many of the underdeveloped nations, as we have seen, impose stringent restrictions on foreign capital; a few are outright hostile to foreign investments. A bold United States program to reimburse its foreign investors against political loss might overcome much of this risk. But there is still, unfortunately, another handicap. The field of *profitable* investment, for foreign capital as well as for domestic capital, is typically restricted in the backward lands. Hence economic as well as political considerations tend to militate against a large and varied private investment effort from the advanced nations, particularly in those areas which are still struggling to gain a first firm foothold on the long ascent.

Foreign aid

And so we pass to the last of the means by which the advanced nations can assist the process of economic development—international aid. And with this we move into

[9] January, 1956, p. 103.

an area which sharply differentiates our own times from the past. International trade and foreign private investment are, after all, as old as ancient Egypt or Rome. But the deliberate transfer of wealth from rich nations to poor for the express purpose of bringing the poor toward a closer parity with the rich is something quite new under the sun.

Partly because it is so new, foreign aid is an untidy subject. It includes, not only country-to-country transactions such as the United States Alliance for Progress program for Latin America, but also multilateral transactions such as those of the World Bank or the various UN agencies. It includes both outright gifts and "hard" and "soft" loans.* It covers military as well as nonmilitary purposes. And in the present competition to "look good" as a contributor to economic development, some European countries do not hesitate to pass off as "foreign aid" purely commercial loans or guarantees.

Hence it is not easy to estimate the amount of nonmilitary capital which, whether in loan or grant form, actually flows from the developed into the underdeveloped world by way of "foreign aid." UN statisticians place the total flow at just under five billion dollars a year, not including the rather small amount of direct Russian aid. This is about double the figure of ten years ago. Remarkably enough, foreign aid with all its political uncertainties has been a more stable source of development help to the underdeveloped countries than world trade.

* A "hard loan" is one which is repayable in the currency of the lender and which therefore absorbs some of the foreign exchange earnings of the borrower. A "soft" loan is repayable in the domestic currency of the borrower—an American dollar loan to India, for example, being paid off in rupees.

At first look, the aid figure is surprisingly small. We tend to think of foreign aid as a massive operation, and it comes as a disconcerting realization to ascertain its modest dimensions. For certainly, measured against the monumental problem of underdevelopment as a whole, the flow of foreign aid seems insignificant. The five billion dollars a year amount to no more than 2 or 3 percent of the total output of the underdeveloped world, to less than 15 percent of its total export earnings.

Yet it is not small in relation to one still more critical figure—the amount of new capital which the underdeveloped nations manage to accumulate each year. *Foreign aid amounts to nearly 30 percent of all capital formation in the underdeveloped world,* excluding only mainland China. This is tantamount to saying that without the supplement of foreign aid the underdeveloped nations would be building only enough new capital to maintain their precarious standards against the dilution of population growth. Whatever small advances are being won against that terrible solvent are due to the margin of new capital which international assistance supplies.

Can the flow of foreign aid be substantially increased?

There can be no doubt that it lies within the capacity of the Western world to increase its contribution very substantially. The United States' total commitment for economic development, stripped of its military component, does not yet amount to half of one percent of its Gross National Product and the commitments of its European allies are considerably less than this. The total amount of UN disbursements is still almost triflingly small: UNICEF, for example, works on an annual budget which would not begin to cover the welfare expenditures of New York City

114

alone; the total expenditures of the UN Special Fund around the world are less than the United States spends on its Indian reservations. What has held back the flow of aid is clearly not the ability but the willingness of the West to give or lend its wealth to the underdeveloped nations.

By how much the flow of international assistance can be raised will thus depend in large part upon the internal politics of the Western world. Suppose, however, that the proposed American-European economic alliance is finally consummated, and that domestic opposition to vastly increased aid dwindles to an ineffectual minority. It might then be possible for the Atlantic Community to generate a surplus of ten to twenty billions a year for investment in the underdeveloped areas.

This is not where matters end, however. Whether such a vast surplus could be invested in the underdeveloped lands is another question. At least in the foreseeable future, to pour such enormous sums into nations which are struggling to find and prepare and staff the individual projects of development would merely speed up an inflationary process which in many underdeveloped countries is already very nearly out of control. Between 1950 and 1960, for instance, the price level in Argentina rose tenfold, in Chile twentyfold, in Bolivia a hundredfold. To open the floodgates of international expenditure too quickly would, unhappily, only accelerate this near-disastrous process.

Thus what is tragic about the present situation is that, with the best will in the world and with unlimited funds, there is a limit as to the amount of aid which most underdeveloped nations can now absorb. For example, India's ambitious third Five-Year Plan contemplates the expenditure of only $23 billion for development *over the next five years,* and of this sum only six billion dollars is specifically dependent upon outside assistance. Yet in the opinion of many economists, this plan, so frighteningly modest when measured against India's needs, may in fact go *beyond* her actual capacity to mobilize and direct men and money.

Hence the degree to which we can realistically raise the sights for international assistance in the near future is not so very great, a fact often overlooked by observers who are appalled at the slow pace of development and who suggest that a "crash program" could do the trick faster. What they fail to ask is how this money could be spent. Assume, for instance, a five-year crash program of ten billion dollars for Africa. Assume further, that nine-tenths of this sum would be spent for machinery bought in America and Europe and only one-tenth spent for labor in Africa. If the average wage paid to an African is $200 a year (a good deal higher than the prevailing wage level), this would mean the engagement of one million Africans, or 10 to 20 percent of its entire available labor force. Who is to organize this colossal working force? On what projects are its energies to be expended? What is going to happen to the price level of Africa's inadequate supply of food under this torrent of added purchasing power? These questions, rarely faced by the ardent proponents of "all-out" aid, give one some idea of the difficulties which must be faced. In fact, the only way in which such a program would be feasible would be virtually to take over a country; to mobilize and organize its labor resources from top to bottom; to impose the most stringent controls and sanctions. This may be the way that an underdeveloped nation eventually lifts itself out of the pit. But it is hardly a way for which a Western nation would have the stomach, or for which any African country would be a willing subject.

To raise these considerations is most emphatically not to deny the immediate efficacy of a good deal more aid, nor the need to press energetically against those barriers which constrict the much wider usefulness of aid. Without question, more can and should be done than is now being done: transfers of foodstuffs on a mass scale, for example, are an obvious way of alleviating the inflationary strains of industrialization which has as yet scarcely been tried. The possibilities for shipping abroad secondhand machinery and vehicles, as well as secondhand consumers items, have never been thoroughly investigated. Then, too, when we consider the amount of misdirected investment even in the most advanced nations, some of the niceties of our criteria for foreign aid projects become quite ridiculous. Surely it is better to proceed with such vigor that some foolish projects get undertaken rather than with such caution that some useful projects are left undone.

But the point is that with all the energy and generosity in the world there is a limit as to what can be accomplished at the moment. Furthermore, that limit is not wildly beyond the present scale of effort, given not only the realistic absorptive capacities of the underdeveloped world, but also the realities of Western politics.* Hence it seems il-

* Under totalitarian discipline, in both giving and receiving countries, no doubt much larger, even huge, transfers of resources could be made. Quite aside from the social and political price, the question would then be whether such massive grafts would "take" or whether the result would be social disorganization on a vast scale.

lusory to look for much more than a continuance, perhaps some moderate augmentation, of the present upward trend in international assistance. This would allow us to expect a total annual flow of foreign aid, from all Western and UN sources, in the vicinity of ten billion dollars by 1970. And even that figure may exceed the willingness of the Western world to give and the ability of the East and South to receive.

The total impact

It is time to put together the various factors we have considered and to reconstitute the formula for development. Many of the variables in that formula, as we have discovered, are not capable of dramatic improvement; others are more hopeful; still others unknown. Let us nonetheless ride boldly over the difficulties by introducing optimistic values wherever they are not totally unrealistic.

We must begin by stressing again the fact that the economics of development is essentially the economics of capital accumulation. Hence we might take as a bench mark the United States, in which the aggregate value of the capital structure—the value of all residential, commercial, and industrial buildings, equipment, livestock, forests, mines, etc.—was estimated at $1.7 trillion in 1958.[10] This is a stock of wealth equivalent approximately to $10,000 for every man, woman, and child in the nation. The aim of the underdeveloped nations is to amass a sum of capital which will, in the fullness of time, approach some such magnitude.

[10] *Statistical Abstract, U.S. Department of Commerce, 1960,* p. 326.

Of course, this cannot be done at once. Let us only imagine that for the present the underdeveloped regions aspire to no more than a stock of new capital equal to only 10 percent of the American sum, or $1,000 for every inhabitant. Assuming high capital-productivity, this might yield an additional flow of output of $300 to $400 a year, effectively tripling and quadrupling their per-capita incomes.

The present population of the underdeveloped areas, not including mainland China, is in the order of 1½ billion people. Thus the rough size of the additional capital stock toward which they must aspire is 1½ billion times $1,000, or a trillion and a half dollars.

Today the underdeveloped nations are accumulating new capital at the rate of perhaps ten to twenty billion dollars a year. Two-thirds of this is internally amassed and has nothing to do with help from overseas. But let us assume that, as the result of a herculean effort to improve the rate of saving and to increase the efficiency of investments, and as a result of a stabilized and enhanced flow of earnings from trade, foreign investment, and foreign aid, the rate of capital accumulation rises to fifty billion dollars a year. It would then take at least twenty-five years to accumulate the capital sum we have established as our goal.

But this, unfortunately, is not the full development equation. Let us remember that during that quarter century of unprecedented accumulation, population will also be rising. By the mid-1980's the noncommunist underdeveloped world will be coping, not with its present 1½ billion, but with some 2¼ billion inhabitants, perhaps more. Hence the per-capita payout of our enormous sum

119

of capital must be pared away by 50 to 60 percent. At the end of a generation of unremitting effort, average annual incomes in the underdeveloped world would still approximate only about two weeks' income of an average American family.

These disappointing results from extravagantly optimistic assumptions lead to a highly important conclusion: economic development over the next decade or two cannot substantially better the lot of the world's *misérables*. We have seen that the net effect of the last decade of development has been to raise the average monetary income in the backward areas by one dollar a year. If the most sanguine forecasts of the UN economists are justified, that improvement can be increased to two dollars within five to ten years. Over twenty to thirty years, the rate of yearly gain might climb to as much as ten dollars. To be sure, this rate of improvement will be much faster in some countries, such as Mexico or possibly Brazil, and much slower in others, such as Saudi Arabia or Ghana. Nevertheless, taking the underdeveloped world as a whole, the upshot of another generation of effort, on a scale far more intensive and effective than today's, will still be a panorama of life not markedly different from that which characterizes these areas today.

This does not mean that economic development will not be taking place. On the contrary, the framework of a more developed economy of the future should by then begin to be visible in the form of schools and roads and factories. The nucleus of a self-generating capital sector should be much more in evidence than it is today. Still more important, invaluable "non-economic" benefits may have been introduced on a considerable scale: the enormous gift of literacy, a better standard of public health, and the like. Yet the stigmata of poverty—hunger, ragged clothes, miserable housing—are likely still to be nearly as visible and widespread as they are today.

Certainly it is well to stress again the brighter prospects of a few nations who have already crossed the worst of the preindustrialization desert. But in general no amount of hopeful thinking can allow us to obscure the fact that the lot of the many is not that of these few. It is only self-deception which pictures economic development leading *within our lifetimes* to any large and continuous human betterment. That lies still in the distant future. In the meantime this generation of the backward lands will have no alternative but to bear the burdens of the past as they labor for a future they will not live to enjoy.

THE
SOCIAL
COST

VII

Thus our survey of the *economic* possibilities for development comes to a sober end. It is clear that the timetable for development must be a protracted one. Very few of the underdeveloped nations have reached a point of capital accumulation at which anything like a "take-off" seems possible within the near future. For most of them, the next generation will be one of preindustrial rather than industrial building, of preparation rather than of cumulative achievement.

This does not mean, let us repeat and emphasize, that economic development is an impossibility for them. There are no impassable barriers in the way—not even that of population growth. The tasks that lie ahead can be fairly clearly visualized. Agriculture must be rationalized, not only in order to lay the basis for a sound agricultural economy, but also to free men for work on capital projects. Great social capital projects must be undertaken with this labor in order to prepare the field on which further advance can be made. Industrial capital must then be built, initially leaning heavily on imports financed by trade and aid, then in time building from its own productive capacities. Meanwhile a development plan must seek to coordinate activities, assigning priorities to various economic salients which hopefully will bring into being new productive possibilities as these are needed.

Yet there is one question which this economic blueprint for development does not answer—or, for that matter, even ask. It is: *who is going to do the developing?* Until we have answered this question we have not fully examined the dynamics of the development process nor fully assessed the costs of the Great Ascent.

The developers

Can private enterprise be the agent of development? Can the great social and economic transformations of the development process be left to the motive power of the profit principle and the restraint of market competition? After all, this was in large degree how the West developed during the eighteenth and nineteenth centuries. Cannot the same agencies of development be applied again to the East and South?

The suggestion has a natural appeal to the Western nations themselves. Unfortunately, those who urge the underdeveloped nations to tread the proven path of the West tend to forget some of the differences between the situation faced by the Western world in its developmental era and that facing the backward nations today.

For the West did not enter upon its period of industrialization in the drastic and abrupt fashion with which the underdeveloped lands seek to make their own transition. On the contrary, a long period of preparation preceded the commencement of the industrial era in the West. From the fourteenth century on, a feudal, nonmonetized, traditional society gave way gradually to a capitalist, monetized, market society. Meanwhile an even longer period of preparation brought the West to a condition of readiness on other fronts, cultural, social, and political.

Most of the backward lands must begin their leap into industrialization without such a period of preparation. Their traditional societies have not melted away before the thaw of a slow monetization. They are, in the main, unaccustomed to the market orientation of life. Their basic social institutions, their political frameworks, their cultures are in a state of flux rather than one of essential stability. Hence economic development comes to them not as the culmination—however difficult—of a long process of social evolution, but as a discontinuous jump from one form of social system to another, radically dissimilar one.

Then, too, the West began its developmental march from a position of pre-eminence vis-à-vis the rest of the world. Militarily and commercially, the West was a predatory group of nations; indeed, the gains from piracy contributed not a little to England's initial developmental burst. By way of contrast, the East and South begin the development climb from a position of inferiority, of victimization, of discrimination. They must fight against world economic pressures in order to develop, rather than riding with them.

In addition, they must fight against internal handicaps of a unique sort. The West did not begin its ascent from a condition of overpopulation. Malthus' warnings notwithstanding, nothing like the Malthusian pressures of the contemporary world undercut their development effort. Modern science did not, within the span of ten years, impart a deadly impetus to their populations. The contrast with the developing areas today could not be stronger. Whereas the West could afford to take its time, the new countries cannot.

Finally, the underdeveloped countries, who are in so many ways strait-jacketed in comparison with the development of the West, have one area of freedom which the West did not enjoy. They have the possibility of a *choice* in economic systems—a choice which did not exist in the eighteenth and nineteenth centuries. The Western nations, as they vied with one another for industrial supremacy, nonetheless all followed a single economic design—that of more or less free enterprise combined with more or less government protection and stimulation. The idea of an economy totally planned and regimented for growth was not yet known and therefore did not offer itself as an alternative. But this option is open to the underdeveloped lands, and it has, as we shall see, powerful appeals.

All these crucial points of difference indicate the difficulties of comparing the condition of underdevelopment today with that in the Western past, or in suggesting that the proper course for the backward nations is to seek to duplicate the Western experience. And then, in addition to these problems is yet another. This is the extreme degree of risk which attends a private enterpriser who seeks to launch a new enterprise in the underdeveloped areas. In a developed economy such as our own, an ambitious businessman opens a new business because he is reasonably confident that he can tempt enough of the general purchasing power of the market to his product to justify his investment. But the would-be enterpriser of the backward world has no such reasonable assurance. Rather than a huge pool of active demand, he faces a thin trickle of purchasing activity. Hence the businessman who steps to the front may well be rewarded for his pains with nothing but painful losses.

This does not mean that private capital formation cannot take place, for indeed it is an important agent of development. But it points out that the role of private capital investment is apt to be less impelling in the underdeveloped lands than it was in the much more dynamic environment of the developing West. In the underdeveloped lands, the capitalist tends to follow development rather than to lead it. Although he is eager enough to avail himself of a profitable opportunity once it has appeared, he is not so apt to be the pioneering influence which spearheads development.

Inevitably in an environment in which inhibitions of a traditional mercantile rather than industrial outlook and handicaps of hard conditions combine to hold back vigorous business leadership, a major share of the industrialization impetus must come from the government. That is, development will only proceed, even at a slow pace, if it is *planned* by some nonbusiness authority. Hence we find central government authorities assuming the pivotal role in every underdeveloped nation. As Wilfred Malenbaum, an authority on Indian development, has put it:

> In India, as in other underdeveloped countries, government must ... undertake many specific operations which in the United States, for example, belong distinctly within the scope of the private businessman. The reasons for this ... stem from the thinness of the supply of entrepreneurship—even in India which is more blessed in this regard than are other poor countries. There is also the difficulty of raising enough funds privately for really big industrial investments like steel mills. Of major importance, moreover, is the fact that there have been decades of relative inaction by the private business sector. ... [The Indian businessman] is less sensitive to the new as a spur for improving the old. Be this as it may, government will need to fill a broad big business leadership role in India.[1]

The problem, however, only begins with this recognition of the indispensable role of government. In theory there is no reason why a mixed economy, not unlike that of, say, Brazil or India, could not *in time* produce the capital needed to mount the full Ascent. Any number of theoretical studies have mapped out the possibilities for government-business partnerships in which economic advance is engineered partly by public action and partly by private enterprise.[2] In the limited number of countries which have a chance of demonstrating impressive development results within a short span of years, this may indeed be the mechanism of progress.

---

[1] Quoted in Higgins, *op. cit.*, pp. 47-48.
[2] See especially the volume by Nurkse previously cited and *The Strategy of Economic Development* by Albert O. Hirschman (New Haven, Yale University Press, 1960).

But for most of the underdeveloped world, where the time horizon for development stretches into the indefinite future, the projection of a mixed economy, half capitalist, half socialist, overlooks one crucial factor. This is the social and political tension of development—a tension which threatens to press the mild solution of a mixed economy toward a much more rigidly controlled political and economic structure.

Social tensions

We have already noted many of the changes which economic development imposes on, and requires from, a society. Illiterate peasants must be made into literate farmers. Defeated slum dwellers must be made into disciplined factory workers. Old and powerful social classes must be deprived of ancient privileges; new and untried social classes must be saddled with enormous responsibilities. Above all, an all-embracing, unremitting drive to change the pattern and tempo of economic life must absorb the labor and thought of the developing nation for an indefinite period.

From our vantage point, in which all of these alterations of life are part of our remote history, we tend to forget how profoundly dislocating, how *revolutionary,* such changes are. To take but one instance, when we approach the question of the rationalization of agriculture, we tend to slough off the problem as one which can be solved by "land reform." But we forget that land reform, for nations in which landownership is the central pillar of the structure of social privilege, is not a small concession to be wrung from landlording groups, but a profound and wrenching alteration of the very basis of wealth and power. We can better imagine the ease with which it may be accomplished by supposing that *we* were an underdeveloped country and that some superior power offered us aid on the condition that we would undertake "share reform"—that is, the redistribution (or even the abolition) of our present concentrated ownership of corporate securities. How rapidly would our own powers-that-be acquiesce in such a proposal? How rapidly will Latin America, where 10 percent of the people own 90 percent of the land, acquiesce in land reform?

We know, for instance, that in Mexico, where land reform was instituted in 1916, only *6 percent* of all the land on the farms was redistributed during the first eighteen years of "reform." In Bolivia land reform required a violent revolution in 1952. Or again, in Guatemala land reform required a revolution—of such left-wing tendencies that the United States was frightened into overthrowing the government which instituted the reform; under the subsequent right-wing government land reform has come to a virtual halt.

"What are the chances for 'peaceful, democratically planned' reforms?" asks Thomas F. Carroll, in a recent essay for the Twentieth Century Fund. He answers:

The available evidence is not encouraging. In fact, on the basis of past experience alone, an outlook of pessimism is warranted. With the possible exception of Venezuela, policy tends to polarize on one side in a "do nothing" attitude and on the other in a radical, revolutionary stance. The former group may tinker with some land settlements or tax reforms, and is likely to appoint commissions to "study the problem." It may even pass some laws—which, however, are likely to remain on the books. With this group in general, the hope is that the problem will go away.[3]

Land reform is not, of course, the only source of grave social friction. With how much avidity will the governments of even the so-called "socialist" nations welcome the rise of trade unions, with their demands for higher wages, as a concomitant of development? Perhaps even more important, with what endurance, what tolerance of frustration, what social attitudes will the *misérables* themselves, the peasants and urban workers of the underdeveloped lands, suffer the long gantlet of development?

For it is well to bear in mind that development is the foe of the great ally of the present social order in all these nations—apathy. As change begins to manifest itself, as the ideas of development trickle down from leaders to followers, a terrible change begins to take place: the underdog wakens to his lowly position. And even if his lot improves—at the rate of two or five dollars a year—he may well feel a new fury if his *relative* well-being is impaired. Thus Oscar Lewis writes of Mexico, one of the fastest developing nations:

... in 1956 over sixty percent of the population were still ill fed, ill clothed and ill housed, forty percent were illiterate, and forty-six percent of the nation's school children were not going to school.... Although the national wealth had greatly increased since 1940, and there had been some rise in the standard of living of the general population, the wealth is unevenly

<hr>

[3] *Latin American Issues,* ed. Albert O. Hirschman (New York, Twentieth Century Fund, 1961), p. 200.

distributed, and the disparity between the lives of the rich and the poor is even more striking than before. Manuel German Parra, a leading Mexican economist, has shown that in 1955 one-hundredth of the gainfully employed population took sixty-six percent of the national income, while the remaining ninety-nine percent received only thirty-four percent; in 1940 the distribution had been exactly the reverse.[4]

Commenting on the condition of the urban poor in his *Children of Sanchez*, Lewis writes:

Indeed the political stability of Mexico is grim testimony to the great capacity for misery and suffering of the ordinary Mexican. But even the Mexican capacity for suffering has its limits, and unless ways are found to achieve a more equitable distribution of the growing national wealth, and a greater equality of sacrifice during the difficult period of industrialization we may expect political upheavals, sooner or later.[5]

Hence, along with improvement in economic standards can come social tensions which were formerly dormant or even nonexistent. We would do well to recall the strains of the early Industrial Revolution in England, with its widening chasm between proletariat and capitalist, when we project in our minds the possible course of affairs in the developing countries today.

Thus it is not only wrong, but dangerously wrong, to pic-

[4] "Mexico since Cardenas," *Social Research*, Spring, 1959, p. 26. The extreme skewness of these figures suggests that they are based solely on monetary payments and do not include the incomes in kind of the small peon. The trend toward increasing inequality is, however, significant, and has been confirmed by other studies.

[5] *The Children of Sanchez* (New York, Random House, 1961), pp. xxx-xxxi.

ture economic development as a long, invigorating climb from achievement to achievement. On the contrary, it is better imagined as a gigantic social earthquake. As Eugene Black has pointed out, we delude ourselves with buoyant phrases such as "the revolution of rising expectations" when we describe the process, rather than the prospect, of development. To many of the people involved in this earthquake, the great social transformation of development is apt to be marked not by rising expectations but by a loss of traditional expectations, not by enjoyable gains but by a new awareness of deprivation.

The political possibilities

All these unsettling considerations converge in one direction. They point to the all-important role of political leadership in inaugurating, guiding, containing, and controlling the comprehensive process of change which development entails. Only political leadership of the most forceful kind can inspire the sacrifice, cajole or command the painful social adaptation, win the confidence—often the blind confidence—needed to carry the Great Ascent along.

But this leadership must be generated in a highly undeveloped political environment. In most backward areas, the sources of political rule are few. In the main the traditional ruling class tends to be of feudal or aristocratic heritage, even more than of strictly business interests. It is generally opposed by a group of highly idealistic, often

132

left-wing intellectuals and political leaders; while "center" opinion tends more often than not to be located in the military, who in any event often provide the main source of stable hierarchical organization. In such an atmosphere political power is strongly polarized and widely separated in viewpoint, and economic development becomes a means, not of promoting consensus, but of exacerbating political frictions and widening the gap between political views.

To many of the existing governments in the underdeveloped lands, particularly those of a semifeudal kind (and this includes most of Latin America as well as the Near East), the prospects of development are at most only halfheartedly embraced. Far better than we, their privileged classes sense the revolutionary potentials which the momentum of economic development could release; and they are loath to initiate the vast projects, the all-out effort by means of which a full-fledged development process could begin. Economic development thus becomes associated, not merely with political "reform" of a mild sort, but with political change of a highly charged kind, in which whole social classes can be destroyed and basic institutions remodeled.

As Professor Edward Mason has written:

Existing social relationships, income distributions, individual values, and human motivations are so inhibiting to economic development of any sort; and the existing governments so unwilling to, or incapable of, initiating change, that it is hard to see how the elementary preconditions of development can be established short of political revolution. And it seems unlikely, if political revolution does occur, that it will bring to power

133

governments dedicated to the promotion of economic development along nineteenth century lines.[6]

The logic of collectivism

Thus inherent to the process of economic development is the latent potential of revolutionary upheaval. As in all such unstable situations it is impossible to generalize as to when—or even whether—the latent forces will become active. Although development is the foe of apathy, history proves abundantly that the forces of inertia are vastly more powerful than those of upheaval, and it may yet be that some developing nations will manage to avoid the travails and bloodshed of violent social change—as did, for example, England during the miseries of the Industrial Revolution.

We should not entertain overly hopeful expectations in this regard, however. In nations which are beset by a desire to catch up, the tendencies for revolutionary change are apt to be much greater than in those which formed the vanguard of history. If social change is not rapid—if the progress of the Great Ascent lags or is purposely slowed down to avoid social stress—a new source of revolutionary disturbance is likely to originate in dissident political groups, whether communist or merely anti-*status quo*.

Hence, we must reckon with the likelihood that over the coming two or three decades, as the pressures grow and the difficulties assert themselves, the guidance of develop-

[6] *Economic Planning in Underdeveloped Areas* (New York, Fordham University Press, 1958), p. 27.

ment will fall into the hands of dedicated revolutionary groups. Mild men will not ride the tigers of development. Neither will mild political or economic systems contain or impel it.

In most of the underdeveloped nations the choice for the command post of development is apt to lie between a military dictatorship and a left-wing civilian dictatorship. (The difference may not be very great, since many of the younger army officers have shown strong left-wing tendencies themselves.) In any event, as Professor Mason writes, the route chosen by the revolutionary developmental elites is not apt to be that of democratic capitalism. Given the inevitable slow pace of development, the heightening of social tensions, and the inescapable rigors of the Great Ascent, the logic of events points to the formation of economic systems and political regimes which will seek to *impose* development on their peoples.

But even the most rigorous governments can speed up development only by so much. The first great projects of social capital formation, with their brigades of labor, lend themselves easily to centralized dictatorship, and, given adequate foreign assistance, the creation of an effective industrial structure can be considerably accelerated by a ruthless concentration on strategic sectors. Yet the pace of over-all progress will still have to be hobbled to the sluggish pace of social change, especially in the recalcitrant peasant villages, and it will still have to cope with the population problem, which may prove intransigent even before totalitarian methods. Above all, the necessity to hold down the level of consumption—to force savings—in order to free resources for the capital-building process will make for a rising level of frustration even under the sternest discipline.

This frustration will almost surely have to be channeled into directions other than that of economic expectations. Hence a deliberately heightened nationalism, a carefully planned ideological fervor, even military adventures are a likely by-product of development. Indeed, in some nations only by marshaling sentiments for such ends may the energies of the peoples be contained and controlled. Thus China endlessly exercises the sentiments of anti-Americanism; Indonesia rattles the saber over the useless jungles of New Guinea; the African states eye each other suspiciously.

In a word, economic development has within it the potential, not alone of a revolutionary situation, but of heightened international friction. Much of this, no doubt, will be of a minor nature, comparable to the Indian march into Goa. Nevertheless economic development will continue to agitate the international scene, and will not, as is sometimes easily asserted, constitute a new force for world peace.

The possibilities for communism

Everything that we have said brings us inevitably to the crucial relationship of communism to economic development—a relationship which, it must now be apparent, is a profoundly deep-rooted one.

It is clear that in the political turmoil of development conditions are often propitious for a communist coup. But if communism were a threat only because of its conspiratorial proclivities, the problem might not be so serious. What is much more important is that communism has a *functional* attractiveness to the underdeveloped lands— that it may be the political and economic system best adapted to the tasks of the backward areas.

There is no secret about the communist blueprint for development. It advocates doing only what every under-developed nation must do: reorganizing agriculture to achieve a surplus of food; transferring this surplus to workers who have been released from agriculture; relentlessly, continuously, single-mindedly using these workers to create capital. The difference is that communism, at least in theory, allows the job to be done with much less of the inertia and friction which hamper it in a non-communist society. Where land is needed, it is taken; where workers are needed, they are moved; where opposition occurs, it is liquidated; where dissent arises, it is suppressed. In place of entrepreneurs who may hesitate for fear of losses, it provides factory managers who are given orders to build. In lieu of a government which must accommodate the claims of the old order against those of the new, it establishes a government whose only orientation is to the future.

One need hardly point out that there is a long distance between theory and practice. Communist economic development has not been smooth or easy. We have seen many cases of partial communist failure, particularly in the reorganization of agriculture.* But these failures must be

* As a consequence of these failures we have increasingly witnessed the growth of diversity among communist economies. A considerable gulf today separates the economic system of Yugoslavia from that of Poland, Poland from Russia, Russia from China. Needless to say, this growing diversity of techniques enhances the relevance and attractiveness of communism to the underdeveloped nations.

compared against the greater failure which exists in the first instance—that is, the virtual absence of *any* development in many of the backward lands.

And here it is important to recognize that, with all its shortfalls, the communist record has been an impressive one. There is much talk in the West of the deceitfulness of communism—of its willingness to divert the attention of the masses from their hardships with wild promises and charges, of its propensity to falsify figures, to invent lies, to distort the intent and actions of the West. All this may be true enough. But when communism promises economic growth, it is on much stronger ground. China, at least until its recent agricultural catastrophe, was probably growing twice to three times as fast as India,[7] and if it can survive its food crisis, it is likely to do so again. Nor should we forget that Russia, now a contender for the industrial supremacy of the world, was, only two generations back, a nation at a stage of development no higher than, say, Brazil or Turkey today. Communism may well be the quickest possible way out of underdevelopment, and the desperate fact is that in many areas of the world the present non-communist effort looks like the slowest possible way.

We have already noted that there is nothing mysterious about the communist techniques for forcing growth. *Rather, what is crucial is that communism, as an ideology and as a practical political movement, is prepared to undertake the revolutionary reorganization of society*—a task before which the noncommunist governments shrink.

---

[7] Cf., e.g., A. Doak Barnett, *Communist Economic Strategy: The Rise of Mainland China* (National Planning Association, Washington, D.C., 1959), p. 11.

To the West, it is this very revolutionary ruthlessness which is the intolerable aspect of communism. And it is not alone the attack on vested interests which arouses Western antipathy. The contemptuous rejection of all noncommunist thought, the icy certitude of communist dogma, its machine-like methods, all repel the West, as do, too, the depressing standards of life so far achieved under communism.

But this is not necessarily the effect produced upon the peoples of the East and South. Never having known political freedom, the hungry peasant and city laborer do not regret its absence. Accustomed to brutality and indifference from the upper classes, the common man submits to the whip of new masters with resignation. Already bent under a heavy yoke, he will bear the still heavier burdens of communism (for communism will surely squeeze him harder and drive him faster than noncommunism), if he can see a chance of lifting the incubus of the past from the shoulders of his children and grandchildren. Even the economic realities of the present communist nations, with their drab living standards, are apt to appear more "real," much closer to imaginable achievement, even more psychologically appealing, to the common man of the backward areas than the gaudy and fantastically removed way of the life of the West.

To set forth these considerations is not to prophesy that communism is the path which the developing lands must "inevitably" follow. Even among the revolutionary leadership elites of the underdeveloped countries, few *wish* to follow the orthodox communist pattern. Other than the hard-core communist cadres, the radical leadership in the backward nations entertains no illusions as to the benefits of a junior partnership in the Sino-Soviet bloc. Hence it is at least possible—and, needless to say, desirable—that the extreme tasks of development may be carried through without subordinating the emerging nations to the ideological and political domination of the communist movement. This is a matter about which it is impossible to make blanket predictions; in the contest between the preferences of the developing elites and the pressures of the developmental situation, the decisive vote may be cast by many factors—the resistance of the Old Orders, the rise of an inspired political leader and his own ideological predilections, the success of noncommunist revolutionary groups in combining discipline with enthusiasm, the blunders—or successes—of the local communist organization.[8]

Whether or not the revolutionary regimes of development are finally pushed into the communist orbit, however, there is no doubt that these regimes will identify themselves as being within the *socialist* orbit. It must be noted that almost without exception every developing nation has dedicated itself to "socialism" from Cuba and China on one extreme, through Mexico and India, even to the recent right-wing government of Syria.

As these examples indicate, volumes could be written today on the variety of systems which pass themselves off as socialist. What is clear, however, is that everywhere in the underdeveloped world the word has a charismatic ring. And it is not merely the clarion syllables, with their over-

[8] For an astute and balanced statement on the applicability and attractiveness of orthodox Soviet techniques to underdevelopment, see A. Nove, *The Soviet Economy* (New York, Frederick A. Praeger, 1961), pp. 303-6.

tones of social justice, which account for the ubiquity of the socialist term, but also a common functional idea—the superiority of a planned to an unplanned economy as a vehicle for providing rapid growth.

Thus the inner tensions of the development revolution promise the appearance of "socialism" on a world-wide scale, a fact which presents the capitalist West with a wholly new environment. That even the milder forms of this socialism will have to contend with powerful forces making for authoritarianism and collectivistism is, as we have seen, a likely prospect for the future. Whether or not the trend will go "all the way," however, does not depend entirely on internal factors. In part it hinges on the response of the West to the challenge of development. What that all-important response may be is the question to which we must now turn.

THE
CHALLENGE TO
THE WEST

VIII

These are the terms on which the challenge of the Great
Ascent is offered to America and the West. It need hardly
be said that they are not the terms we ordinarily envisage.
For the realities of the development process directly question the two main premises on which American public
opinion has been based. They make it clear that economic
development is not a process which commands the uncomplicated allegiance of our humanitarian impulses. And
they make it equally clear that economic development
does not directly lead to a state of world affairs easily iden-
tified with American world interests.

These are distressing and even bewildering considerations. It is one thing to encourage public approval for economic development as a kind of international charity, and
another to see in it an agency of deliberate sacrifice,

whether of today's generation in the name of tomorrow's, or of tomorrow's in the name of today's. So too it is one thing to engage America in the world-wide struggle for development on the assumption that a successful Great Ascent will strengthen the forces of democracy and capitalism, and another to ask it to engage itself in a struggle whose successful end-result is apt to be a growth of political authoritarianism and economic collectivism.

Of course, one hopes for an attack on the problem of world poverty which will combine the dedication and the willingness to undertake monumental tasks of the revolutionist with the tolerance and open-mindedness of the humanist. One hopes for a program of development which will judiciously temper the need for sacrifice with a compassion for those who must make the sacrifice. But what if such combinations are not available? What if the inherent obstacles of waging a campaign against stagnant social orders naturally bring to the fore revolutionaries of narrow minds and cruel appetites? What if tolerance and open-mindedness prove to be qualities incompatible with the iron discipline needed for a rapid escape from the pit? What then?

There are no easy answers to such grinding questions. The harsh prospects and problems of development sweep away the satisfying identification of self-interest with altruism and leave in its place only the unsatisfying necessity to choose the lesser among inescapable evils. And what is true for our private moral determination is no less true for our public decisions as a nation. There are no responses on the part of our government which will make of development a benign process whose outcome naturally accords with American ideals and institutions. On the contrary, the realization forced upon us by economic development is that our power to shape the context of the future is much less than it has been in the past. Economic development, with its immense drive and its dangerous proclivities, places us in a defensive position in which our freedom of maneuver is necessarily limited.

It is not, of course, totally gone. Limited intervention in the future, as in the past, may enable us to bolster friendly but shaky governments or to unseat inimical and shaky regimes. But the presence of the Russian and Chinese counterforce makes it unlikely that military action can exert more than a marginal restraint on revolution in the more distant underdeveloped world, while in Latin America anti-American sentiments may make even of diplomatic intervention a risky and possibly disastrous course of action. The probabilities are great that we shall have to stand more or less impotently by while the dynamics of development work their troubled way, "surrounding" us in Asia, Africa, and South America with governments whose policies and programs point in a general direction counter to that which we ourselves desire.

The threat of isolationism

If active intervention to repress the revolutionary tendency of development is apt to be largely denied to us, another possibility remains. It is not inconceivable that the untoward drift of world affairs will give rise to powerful voices urging a Western—and, in particular, American—disengagement from the underdeveloped world, a curtailment of aid, a turning away from active participation in or support for the Great Ascent.

It is an uncertain question as to how far the Western economies *can* sever their connections with the raw material producers of the backward continents. There is no question at all, however, that such a course would make things incalculably worse for the West. All the adverse trends latent within the underdeveloped lands would be vastly accelerated were America to turn its back on development. If we cannot easily divert or contain the revolutionary consequences of development despite generous assistance, we certainly cannot prevent them by refusing aid. The revolutions will take place whether we offer money or not; and if the immediate pace of advance would be slowed down, were we to turn aside, the wrath and disorder of the development revolution would only be increased. To some extent Russia can supply the materials we would refuse. Unquestionably, she would be the immense beneficiary of world sentiment and political orientation. In the international arena, isolationism would spell the decline of American world influence—an influence which, as we shall see, can still be exercised to some advantage.

Even more self-defeating would be the moral effect of isolation at home. After all, the Western nations are an immense reservoir of wealth in an impoverished world. In America we have enormous surpluses of food which embarrass us while the world's belly aches from emptiness. We have excess capacity in many industries while in the backward lands the pace of progress creeps for lack of machines and materials of every kind. We have skills and talents which go begging or are frittered away in second-rate employments while the underdeveloped continents cry out for expertise of every kind. We throw on the junk heap vehicles which would furnish invaluable transportation to a world which still totes much of its burdens on its backs; we discard outmoded wardrobes which would clothe men and women who have never known what it was like to have an unused garment; we spend in night clubs a sum which would cover the national budgets of a dozen pinched nations. Not to use this abundance for the betterment of mankind would be evidence of a moral decay as destructive of the West as any number of external revolutions.

And then there is a final thought. The political prospect of an isolated America—even an isolated West—is not a reassuring one. A beleaguered fortress of privilege, its doors closed and its walls manned, does not tend to nurture wise and tolerant government. To live in fear of the developing world, to count its successes as our defeats, to feel the rush of the history-making process into the vacuum of the East and South as a threatening current, could well encourage the ugliest political possibilities in the West. Isolationism might free us from the need to deal with extremist governments abroad, but it is likely to do so at the price of having to deal with them at home.

Selective support

A much more positive and appealing program would throw us into the struggle for development on a selective basis. That is, it would urge us to concentrate our assistance on those nations which stand a chance of struggling up the mountain of development without resort to totally collectivist, extreme left-wing measures. Mexico, Argentina, Brazil and India have often been proposed as the main objects for such a concentrated program of assistance.*

There is a good deal of justification for channeling our money where the pay-off possibilities are greatest, not only because the successful developers offer the greatest chance for spending that money usefully, but also because they offer us the best chance to keep our *own* morale high. To a certain extent the realities of the development process do in fact result in such a concentration of aid. Yet there are difficulties in the way of adopting this as an "official" policy. For even with the most successful noncommunist developers the outlook is not all propitious. India's fate hangs in the balance, and after Nehru's death it is entirely possible that the nation will fly apart into linguistic fragments and that development along Western lines will go into the discard. Brazil is still racked by revolutionary sentiment in the north. Argentina has recently shown the revolutionary potential that lurks beneath a seemingly firm government. Mexico gives more promise of stability, but we have caught a glimpse of the disturbing possibilities inherent in its proletariat.

And even if all goes for the best in these nations, it will not be easy, or perhaps even possible, to keep aid restricted to them without accelerating an unwanted trend in other nations. What will happen to Pakistan if it is short-changed in comparison with India? Can we help Argentina and not

* Cf. Andrew Schonfield, *The Attack on World Poverty* (New York, Random House, 1960).

Chile, Colombia, Venezuela? And if them, can we ignore Peru and Bolivia? Is it feasible to assist Nigeria but not Ghana? The pressures of political reality almost inevitably impose a diffusion of a would-be concentration of aid. Certainly, it makes sense to bend our first efforts where they are most likely to succeed. But it is doubtful if we can do so to the exclusion of other countries. If we are to have any foreign aid program, it will have to include, to some degree, a wide variety of nations—the less successful developers along with the more successful, the less friendly along with the more friendly.

The premises of political policy

What can we do, then, to live with the revolutionary trend of economic development?

It must be clear that the first essential is not a change in policy so much as a change in point of view. We must lift ourselves out of our accustomed American frame of reference and catapult ourselves across a distance wider than the oceans that separate us from the continents in which the struggle for development is taking place. To repeat a phrase we have used more than once, we must learn to see the Great Ascent as it is, and not as we would like it to be.

From such an altered point of view comes the realization that we can only exert an influence over the direction of economic development, if we use our power in consonance with the drift of events and not against it. In a word, if we are to modify the general direction of the Great Ascent, we can only do so by accepting the need for political authoritarianism and economic collectivism during the early stages of development of many nations. To put the matter in its bluntest terms, *we must forge a foreign policy which begins with the explicit premise that democratic capitalism, as a model for economic and political organization, is unlikely to exert its influence beyond the borders of the West, at least within our lifetimes.*

It need hardly be said that the official articulation of such a premise would present extraordinary difficulties— practical as well as ideological. At home it would expose an administration to the grave political risks of expounding an unpopular and "defeatist" world view to an electorate which has hitherto been led to believe that the Western system had every prospect of expanding—not by force but by force of example. Abroad it would destroy at one blow the simple guideline that automatically equates our national interest with economically "liberal" governments and opposes it to economically collectivist ones.

Ironically, however, such a "defeatist" view is apt to be the most effective means we have to protect our own institutions and to maintain some area of effective influence. For it asks us to recognize that by supporting governments which, for whatever reason, do not accelerate development to the utmost we may be only laying the groundwork for eventual revolutions of uncontrollable tendencies, while in helping governments of unpalatable authoritarian and collectivist hues we may be in fact preventing the rise of something worse. To be sure, this does not mean that tyrannous governments are by virtue of their very repressions the ones which America must support. The infinitely difficult discrimination which a realistic premise for policy enjoins is the need to distinguish between mere oppression and oppressive but purposeful discipline, between static dictatorship and dictatorial development. Very often both will be visible. In that event we shall have to guard against the easy temptation to confuse the rights of property with the rights of man, and thereby to rationalize our support for conservative regimes and our opposition to radical ones.

Above all, an effective policy requires a change in the official attitude of America toward "socialism" in the underdeveloped world. We have already noted that very few, even among the most radical development elites, wish to be pulled into the existing communist orbit. But under the cumulative pressures of the Great Ascent, noncommunist governments may well be forced into that camp unless they receive the strongest possible encouragement—and not merely a grudging acquiescence—in finding independent solutions along indigenous socialist lines.

Our executive and planning staffs have already come a considerable distance toward recognizing the necessity for political authority and economic planning as preconditions for rapid development. But there still remains a long way to go. A long and deep educational process will be needed if enlightened executive policies are to receive legislative support. And then, too, it is not easy to communicate with the leaders of the underdeveloped world so long as powerful private voices continue to give lip service to the pieties and polemics of free private enterprise and democracy in a situation in which all too frequently both are not only totally inapplicable, but would spell chaos or even retrogression. When, for instance, the leadership elites of the backward nations read an editorial in the *New York Times* lamenting the rise of socialism in Egypt and urging that "it is necessary for us in the West to prove that our democratic free enterprise system is better than any variation of socialism,"[1] these leaders feel that important interests in America are willing to consign them to a slower rate of economic growth and a lesser portion of economic justice in defense of their own well-padded system of economic privilege. And insofar as these American interests are suggesting that capitalism rather than socialism should be the main vehicle of development, the leaders of the underdeveloped nations are right.

Thus one consequence of a new view of the realistic possibilities before the majority of the developing countries must be that strategic groups in America learn to speak a new language abroad—certainly not the dogmatics of Marxism-Leninism, but the language of planning, of controls, of social and economic justice. If America wishes to make its counsels heard among the revolutionary elites, its spokesmen must speak the words that answer their questions.

The internationalization of foreign aid

The initial premise of Western foreign policy toward economic development must thus be an acceptance of its revolutionary potentials. Yet it is clear that, even with the best of intentions and most audacious of political leadership, the United States must not expect too much. A rich and privileged nation in a poor and underprivileged world

[1] *New York Times*, August 16, 1961. It is only fair to note that in general the *Times* has been far from doctrinaire in its view of development, particularly by comparison with most American newspapers.

cannot avoid becoming the target of hostilities and frustrations. An anti-Western, anti-American attitude is likely to color the general foreign outlook of most developing nations, regardless of our ability to soften their animosity by a new show of understanding for their internal problems.

This is bound to place America in the difficult position of seeking to extend assistance to nations which are not only authoritarian and collectivist but which are more or less actively anti-American. If we accept this, too, as part of the price of development, then a subsidiary aspect of American policy must be the creation of avenues for assisting development without incurring unacceptable conflicts of immediate interest. That is, we must find ways of speeding development without placing ourselves in the impossible position of directly extending help to nations which are publicly unsympathetic or even unfriendly in their relations with our government.

There is only one way in which this difficult objective can be achieved. More and more of the development effort must be handled by international agencies. The support of development must be placed as much as possible outside the arena of domestic politics.

This is not an aim which can be accomplished overnight. The organizational means for an effective handling of aid on an international basis do not now exist. The present international agencies have not excelled in their administration of aid, erring sometimes on the side of laxness, sometimes (and especially in the case of the World Bank) on the side of overstrictness. To advocate the immediate wholesale transfer of assistance to the United Nations, or even to some new *ad hoc* body of Western nations, would probably result in a considerable diminution of congressional appropriations and would thus be bitterly opposed by the present recipient nations.

Nevertheless it is necessary to think and plan ahead. The tensions and disruptions of the developing world are by no means apt to diminish, as we have sought to demonstrate. If we project the likely revolutionary drift of affairs in the underdeveloped world and consider the problem of assisting governments whose political complexion may well become increasingly distasteful, it is necessary to consider how conflicts of interest can be diluted and buffered, and how aid to development can be continued when it is no longer a "popular" object of public support.

Against this impending possibility there seems to be no adequate response but the internationalization of assistance on a considerably larger scale than that of today. The depoliticizing of foreign aid has already begun with respect to certain aspects of development: health, technical assistance, agricultural research, etc. The World Health Organization, the Technical Assistance Board, the Food and Agriculture Organization already make decisions and administer programs, many of which would be extremely difficult to carry out as "American" projects. Such a transfer of administrative responsibility to international groups, whether under the aegis of the UN or of other agencies, will certainly not remove the conflicts of interest which are inherent in the process of aiding revolutionary governments, but it may well prove to be the best means of holding these conflicts within manageable proportions. This is not, of course, incompatible with the maintenance of direct bilateral aid wherever this continues to offer the smoothest and most fruitful working relationship.

Reform at home

The gradual internationalization of aid may succeed, to some extent, in diluting the hostility which the Great Ascent is likely to stir up at home. It will not, however, affect the hostility which development will surely stir up in the emerging countries themselves. Against this powerful animus, the United States has but one effective response. It must demonstrate to the leaders of the underdeveloped nations that we too have our profound problems, albeit of a different sort, and that we are capable of as much political courage at home as we do not hesitate to ask abroad.

This forces the consideration of a delicate but central problem—that development today is largely a "colored" problem, and that it is taking place in a world which is still dominated by nations many of which regard the colored races as inferior to the white. Here the Western powers, and in particular the United States, must candidly assess their own attitudes. It is an ugly word, but the United States today is a racist nation—not, to be sure, at the center of official government, but emphatically and openly in some of its state governments, and pervasively and silently in the attitudes and actions of the majority of its white population.

And whereas the official policy of the Federal Government is against racial discrimination, its willingness to take risks and fight battles on behalf of this policy has not, to date, been remarkable for its bravery.* To the ,colored

* Although the Justice Department has made an encouraging start during recent months.

154

nations of the world, what is visible in our country is a scale of values which does not inhibit our government from using force to oppose an alien political philosophy but which plucks at its sleeve with a thousand cautions when the internal racial question is raised. On the face of it, racial equality is not an aim for which the United States Government is prepared to run outstanding political risks, an aim which is preached loudly but practiced softly. Until this great flaw is remedied, or at least made the target of courageous and unremitting effort, it will not be easy for America—and to a somewhat lesser degree, for the West at large—to parade as the political ideal on which the black, yellow, and brown nations of the underdeveloped world should model themselves.

There is here an issue still larger than that of racial injustice in itself. It is the issue of demonstrating to the emergent leaders of the world that the United States is still the bearer and the guardian of the ideals of freedom in whose name it was founded. For it is well to recognize that freedom is not the banner under which the West marches, in the eyes of many who see it from the South and East. Those who find the leaders of the underdeveloped world ungrateful or unperceptive for failing to recognize the West as the "champion of freedom" might reflect that Nehru wrote his great book in a British jail,* that most of the leaders of the Indonesian Republic were at one time political prisoners of the Dutch, that the original leaders of the Algerian revolution were shamefully betrayed and incarcerated by the French while traveling on a "safe

* Which is not to deny that he would have been in a communist coffin.

passage," that Guatemala was subverted by American power following its first revolution, that the nations of Africa won their independence against Belgian, French, and British resistance and still struggle against Portuguese colonialism. Country by country, it has been almost without exception the nations of the "freedom-loving" West which have opposed and fought the independence of the new nation-states. If the communists have Korea, Tibet, Hungary, and the Baltic states on their conscience, we have enough on ours.

Hence the task confronting the Western nations is not to maintain but to regain their historic identification with freedom—to win it anew in the eyes of the world. To some extent this can be done by the exercise of a wise, realistic, and generous foreign policy. But to a much more important degree it will have to be done at home. It is idle to pretend that the West can be an effective model for the immediate economic and political development of the backward world. What we must hope and work for is to make it a model for their long-term evolution. The West and America can offer, in the living examples of their societies, meanings of freedom which can exert their powerful attractions for the future: a genuine solicitude for the right of the dissenting individual, a greater concern for the disprivileged individual than for the privileged one, an encouragement of personal life goals that go beyond the mere accumulation of consumers goods. The West may yet be a lodestar for the global revolution which is now only in its incipient stages, but it will hardly succeed in inspiring the world's imagination unless it first succeeds in inspiring its own.

The choice before America

Thus the price of leadership in world economic development comes home to us as a domestic political challenge —perhaps in the end as the supreme domestic political challenge.

It may be that the challenge will be too great. It may be deemed political suicide to speak of problems of development in blunt terms, to force a consideration of unpleasant alternatives and moral dilemmas, to encourage governments whose political and economic structures are alien and even antipathetic to ours. It may appear impractical to urge an internationalization of foreign aid; impolitic to engage in an uncompromising campaign for racial equality; unnecessary to press forward on a hundred difficult fronts of domestic reform. In other words, the actions which are open to us may be open only in theory, in the abstract, and not in hard fact. In that case, if the argument of this book is valid, we must be prepared to bear the consequences of inaction, which is to say, the probable slow loss of prestige and leadership to the communist world.

Whether or not the United States and the West will be capable of risking the heroic course needed to maintain a working influence on the historic transformation of our day is difficult to say. The gulf between conditions in the underdeveloped world and our own is so great that what appears from their point of view as a cautious and conservative program for us to follow appears to us as a daring and radical one. Without question the measures needed to gird the United States against the future—much less to establish its moral leadership in a revolutionary world—will strain to the hilt the adaptability of our social order, both at its centers of power and among the electorates whom it entertains and diverts and semieducates. No one can confront this impending test with an easy assurance as to its outcome.

What is certain is that the price of economic development will not be borne by the developing world alone. Its stresses and strains will have to be faced as well in the advanced countries. Ahead lies a long gantlet through which rich and poor, favored and disfavored alike, must pass; and in that period of trial it is less likely that the poor will falter who have their lives at stake than the rich who may fear for their way of life.

Yet if the Great Ascent is slow, cruel, even fearsome, it is also irresistible, stirring, grandiose. It is an avenue of history which, however difficult, leads from an eternity of dark suffering toward the possibility of light and life. That it will surely usher in a period of disorder, readjustment, even temporary defeat is as true for the fortunate few as for the unfortunate many, but it is also possible to see such a period as prelude to a more distant era in which, for the first time, the potentialities of the entire human race may be explored. Thus if the trial is very great, so is the ultimate prospect. In the end it must be this prospect on which we fix our eyes and hopes if we too are to make our Great Ascent.

INDEX

Africa
    agricultural productivity in, 39
    "crash program" for, 116
    soil conditions in, 33-34
Agriculture (see also Land reform)
    attitude of upper classes to, 49
    low productivity in, 39-42
    rationalization of, 74-81
    trend in output, 89-90
Aid (see Foreign aid)
America, response to development, 10-14, 142-158
Authoritarianism, 20-21, 132-135, 150
Attitudes (see also Social attitudes)
    to capitalism, 67, 133-135, 140
    to development, 64, 69-70, 80, 130-132
    to West, 66-67, 154-155

Barnett, A. Doak, 138n.
Birth control (see Population control)
Black, Eugene, 47, 56, 57, 95, 132
Business class, 48-9, 126-127

Capital (see also Saving, Investment, Foreign investment)
    absence of, 42-43
    accumulation, 74-87, 118-119
    imperialism and, 63-64
    industrial, 77-84, 99
    productivity, 85, 88-89, 94-99, 119
    social, 77-81, 83, 99
    and social structure, 51-52
Capitalism
    attitudes to, of underdeveloped countries, 67, 133-135, 140

Capitalism, Cont.
    and development, 123-127, 133-135, 150-151
    and imperialism, 63-68
Carr, E. H., 9n.
Carroll, Thomas H., 129
Class structure, 51
Climate, 31-32
Collectivism, 20-21, 134-136, 150
Colonialism, 63-68
Committee for Economic Development, 108
Commodity fluctuation, 104-105
Communism
    and development, 136-141, 157
    peasant resistance to, 80
Consumption, 75, 79, 135
Cooperatives, 80
Curle, Adam, 52n.

Development
    and capitalism, 123-127, 133-135, 150-151
    and collectivism, 134-136
    and communism, 136-141
    economic core of, 73-87
    handicaps to, 23-31, 32 ff., 80-81
    imperialism and, 63-67
    "iron law" of, 85-86
    and land reform, 78, 100, 128-130
    lopsided, 65-66
    performance, 89-90
    political problems of, 100-102, 132 ff.
    prospects for, 19-21, 88 ff.
    socialism and, 140-141, 150-151
    social preconditions for, 53, 78

Economic development (see Development)
Egypt
    agricultural production in, 76

Egypt, Cont.
    population growth in, 55-56
Exports
    fluctuations in, 104-108
    as source of capital, 83, 102-103
Extractive industries, 110-111

Foreign aid, 83, 85, 108
    internationalization of, 152-153
    limits to, 115-118
    size of, 112-115
Foreign investment, 83, 108-112
Foreign trade, 102-108
Fortune magazine, 111-112
Frost, Raymond, 104n.

Geography of underdevelopment, 28-31
Government
    attitude to, 50
    controls over saving, 100-102, 135
    planning, 126 ff.
Growth (see Development)
Gunther, John, 41

Hansen, Alvin, 44-45, 46
Higgins, Benjamin, 31, 40, 127n.
Hirschman, Albert, 50, 127n.
Hoffman, Paul, 37, 107n.

Illiteracy, 97
Imperialism, 63-68
India
    and China, 138
    development in, 89-90
    Five Year Plan, 116
    foreign trade, 103
    government planning in, 127
    linguistic problem, 148
    peasant attitudes, 44-45
    population pressure, 56
    primogeniture, 41

159

Indonesia, population pressure in, 56
Industrial capital, 77, 81-84
Industrialization, 81-87, 99
and foreign aid, 112-118
and population control, 93
and trade, 102-104
Inflation, 115
Internationalization of aid, 152-153
Investment, 85-87, 88
(see also Capital, Foreign investment)
"Iron law" of development, 85-87
Isolationism, 144-146
Issawi, Charles, 76n.

Jackson, Sir Robert, 70

Kenen, Peter, 103
Kimble, George, 33n., 39

Labor
attitude of, 47
hidden potential of, 75-81
Land reform, 77-78, 100
revolutionary aspects of, 128-130
Leadership (see Political leadership)
Leibenstein, Harvey, 100n.
Lewis, Arthur, 45
Lewis, Oscar, 50n., 130, 131

Malaria, 58-59
Malenbaum, Wilfred, 90n., 127n.
Mason, Edward, 133-134, 135
McClelland, David, 36n.
Mead, Margaret, 46n.
Mexico
land reform in, 129

Mexico, Cont.
income distribution in, 130-131
Military leadership, 134-136

Nationalism, 67-69, 136
Nationalization, 67
New York Times, 150, 151n.
Nove, Alec, 140n.
Nurkse, Ragnar, 76n., 77n., 79n., 127n.

One-crop economies, 66, 114-118

Parra, Manuel German, 131
Peasant
labor wasted, 75-76
resistance, 80-81
social type, 44-46
Plastrik, Seymour, 92n.
Political leadership, 69, 132 ff.
Population
control, 91-94
growth, 54-57, 70, 89
and "take-off," 85-86
Pre-investment surveys, 96-99
Productivity
of agriculture, 39-42, 74-81
of capital, 42-43, 85, 88-89, 94-99

Racism, 68-69
in United States, 154-155
Rainfall, 32-33
Reform (see also Land reform)
Political, 133
in United States, 154-155
Resources, 33-36

Revolutionary process, 17-18, 128, 132-140
Rollins, C., 111n.
Rostow, W. W., 84

Saving, 74-75, 78, 85-86, 135
raising rate of, 100-102
Schonfield, Andrew, 147n.
Selective support of development, 147-148
Sickness, 58-59
Singer, H. W., 86n.
Skills, 98-99
Small-scale industry, 98-99
Social attitudes, 43 ff., 84
Social capital, 77-81, 83, 99
Socialism, 67, 140-141, 150-151
Social stratification, 51
Standard of living, 23-27

"Take-off," 84-87, 122
Tanganyika, 96-97
Taxation, 79, 101
Technical assistance, 98-99
Terms of trade, 105
Trade, 102-108

Underdevelopment (see also Development)
causes of, 32 ff.
conditions in, 23-27
geography of, 27-31
and imperialism, 63-68
United Nations Special Fund, 97
United Nations Technical Assistance Program, 98, 153

"Vicious circles," 58

World Bank, 101, 152

Young, George, 25n.